Reading and Writing
Literary Genres

Kathleen Buss
University of Wisconsin—Stevens Point
Stevens Point, Wisconsin, USA

Lee Karnowski
University of Wisconsin—River Falls
River Falls, Wisconsin, USA

INTERNATIONAL
Reading Association
800 Barksdale Road, PO Box 8139
Newark, Delaware 19714-8139, USA
www.reading.org

Director of Publications   Joan M. Irwin
Assistant Director of Publications   Jeanette K. Moss
Editor in Chief, Books   Matthew W. Baker
Permissions Editor   Janet S. Parrack
Associate Editor   Tori Mello
Assistant Editor   Sarah Rutigliano
Acquisitions and Communications Coordinator   Amy T. Roff
Publications Coordinator   Beth Doughty
Association Editor   David K. Roberts
Production Department Manager   Iona Sauscermen
Art Director   Boni Nash
Electronic Publishing Supervisor   Wendy A. Mazur
Electronic Publishing Specialist   Anette Schütz-Ruff
Electronic Publishing Specialist   Cheryl J. Strum
Electronic Publishing Assistant   Jeanine K. McGann

Project Editor   Tori Mello

Cover Illustration   Margaret Scott

Library of Congress Cataloging in Publication Data
 Buss, Kathleen.
 Reading and writing literary genres/Kathleen Buss and Lee Karnowski.
  p.   cm.
 Includes bibliographical references and index.
 ISBN 0-87207-257-6
  1. Literature–Study and teaching (Elementary).   2. Literary form–Study and teaching (Elementary).   3. Reading (Elementary).   4. English language–Composition and exercises–Study and teaching (Elementary)   I. Karnowski, Lee.   II. Title.
 LB1575.B87   2000   99-059011
 372.64–dc21

Fifth Printing, August 2003

In memory of my mother,
Regina Telepak, who taught me to read,
and to my husband,
Bruce, who has encouraged me to write.
                              −K.B.

To my mother, Mae Legters,
who read to me,
and to my sons, Mike, Mark, and Eric,
who were read to.
                              −L.K.

Contents

Acknowledgments

All of the units in this book have been piloted in classrooms. The authors would like to thank the teachers who taught these units, all of whom made suggestions to strengthen the units and shared with us their students' written work, some of which we have included in each genre chapter. We would like to thank the following teachers:

Amy Trawicki, Teacher of Third Grade, Marathon Elementary School, Wausau, Wisconsin, USA.

Sheila Scholz, Teacher of Third Grade, John Muir Elementary School, Portage, Wisconsin, USA.

David Hagendorn, Teacher of Third Grade, Lincoln Elementary, Wausau, Wisconsin, USA.

Betsy Wiberg, Teacher of Fourth Grade, Plover Whiting Elementary, Plover, Wisconsin, USA.

Angela Cooper, Teacher of Special Education, Franklin Elementary School, Merrill, Wisconsin, USA.

Steve Van Ark, Teacher of Fifth Grade, Plover Whiting Elementary School, Plover, Wisconsin, USA.

Lori Knepfel, Teacher of Sixth Grade, Plover Whiting Elementary School, Plover, Wisconsin, USA.

Lorna LaPorte, Teacher of Sixth Grade, Tri–County Elementary School, Plainfield, Wisconsin, USA.

Leanne Niemuth, Teacher of Fifth Grade, Sacred Heart School, Polonia, Wisconsin, USA.

Renee Shulfer, Teacher of Sixth Grade, Bannach Elementary School, Stevens Point, Wisconsin, USA.

Kelly Reimer, Teacher of Third Grade, Weaver Elementary School, Oakdale, Minnesota, USA.

Marylyn Sybrant, Teacher of Third Grade, Oak Park Elementary School, Stillwater, Minnesota, USA.

Jennifer Koenning, Teacher of Fourth Grade, Oak Park Elementary School, Stillwater, Minnesota, USA.

Faye Matson and Jean Anderson, Team Teachers of Fifth and Sixth Grade, Oak Park Elementary School, Stillwater, Minnesota, USA.

Nancy McLain, Special Educator for Autistic Children, Prior Lake, Minnesota, USA.

Kathleen Drinkwine, Teacher of Sixth Grade, Battlecreek Elementary School, Battlecreek, Minnesota, USA.

Mary Johnson, Teacher of Third Grade, St. Croix Falls Elementary School, St. Croix Falls, Wisconsin, USA.

Pat LeFever, Teacher of Sixth Grade, Battlecreek Elementary School, Battlecreek, Minnesota, USA.

We would like to express our appreciation to the editors of the International Reading Association for their assistance. Thank you to Matt Baker, Editor in Chief, for his timely insights into what our early drafts could become, and for his encouragement and support as he guided our preparation of this manuscript. Thanks also to Tori Mello, Associate Editor, for her work on this project and for her personal responses to our inquiries that showed how much she cared about this manuscript; she patiently asked those questions that caused us to clarify and extend our thinking. Finally, thank you to the children who graciously contributed their writings and illustrations, and to their parents, who gave permission for us to share their children's work with our readers.

Teaching Literary Genres

Over the last decade we have seen the approaches to teaching reading and writing change dramatically. Instead of using published basal reading series and workbooks to teach reading, many teachers are now using children's literature. Literature–based reading is a generic term used to describe a reading program that employs quality literature and may revolve around themes or genre studies. In a literature–based reading program, students read authentic literature, have some ownership over the books read, and make choices in the way they will respond to their reading.

When teachers started to use literature–based reading, the traditional instructional arrangement of ability grouping was not a viable option. Therefore, practitioners generated instructional arrangements such as reading workshop, literature response groups, and literature circles. These arrangements encouraged reading and responding as the basis for instruction. Thus, the act of reading has become a socially oriented, interactive process that allows for personal responses.

Louise Rosenblatt (1978) introduced reader response and placed response to text on a continuum from text–based (efferent) to reader–based (aesthetic). Both stances should be present in a literature–based classroom because both are important. The efferent side of the continuum is particularly important when our goal is to teach how authors write in the different genres. Corcoran (1992) states that in stories there are particular features such as narrative shifts in setting and time, the construction of major and minor characters, and the significance of repeated events or verbal structures that are important to understanding the genres of literature.

Zarrillo and Cox (1992) helped educators interpret Rosenblatt's theory for use in the classroom by defining instructional strategies that reflect reader response theory. One way to elicit efferent responses from students is to concentrate on analyzing the features of text by focusing instruction on literary elements of characters, setting, style, and story structure. Aesthetic responses to literature can be elicited by allowing students to choose books to read and their responses, to relate associations and feelings, and to extend the text. You can extend the text by offering choices of activities that encourage students to go beyond the basic story line of the books they read. These activities should encourage students to use drama for retelling, to use art for addressing the story elements of setting and characters, to use writing to extend the story line by writing another ending or rewriting scenes, or to use research strategies to find out more about a story's time period or character.

Instruction in writing has been totally revised in the last decade as well. Emerging from the teacher-selected topics and one-draft "finished" products of the past, the concept of process writing has revitalized writing in today's classrooms. Process writing as defined by Donald Graves (1983) follows a recursive pattern of prewriting, drafting, revising, editing, and publishing.

When teachers began to use process writing in the classroom, the traditional method of having every student write a one-draft final copy was no longer an option. Therefore, practitioners generated the instructional arrangement of the writer's workshop, a term coined by Lucy McCormick Calkins (1986) that established a special time set aside for study and participation in the writing process. The writer's workshop is a time when students learn about the craft of writing through exploration and learn how to become authors in their own right. Students select their topics, the audiences, and the form of their writing. A process writing classroom is arranged so that students are free to talk, share, brainstorm, and write, so clusters of students are grouped together and allowed to share their work and use peers as resources. This arrangement promotes a socially oriented interactive experience and ownership of the writing process. Harste, Short, and Burke (1988) developed a model of the writing process that includes invitations to write a specific genre at points within the yearly writing process. This model encourages teachers to demonstrate writing different genres and to encourage the whole class to try each new form.

The idea that reading and writing are interactive rather than separate content areas has changed the way both subjects are viewed. Reading had been viewed as a decoding process and writing as an encoding process, but with the advent of a meaning-centered approach, both subjects are now seen as having the same goal—that of constructing meaning. This idea has led practitioners to use children's literature as a model for writing and to encourage students to use writing as a response to literature. It also has led to teaching reading and writing skills that are similar in content and purpose.

Frank Smith (1983) reminded us that students learn to be better writers from what they read. To do this, they needed to read like writers, engaging with the author. To read like a writer requires that students see the need to learn from the author, which is dependent on whether they see themselves as writers. This idea has led teachers to talk about how authors write, to provide a variety of genres for students to enjoy and learn from, and to encourage all students, regardless of age, to join the "writer's club."

Finally, the idea of understanding different genres as independent entities has become important. Until quite recently, the study of literature was divided into two major types of text structures: nonfiction (expository) and fiction (narrative). Story structure is taught to beginning readers as beginning, middle, and end, and to intermediate students as setting, characters, conflict, attempts to solve the conflict, resolution, and ending. These categories are too broad to reflect adequately the richness and the variations within each genre of text. This book will help provide practitioners opportunities to discuss a variety of text structures and the many elements used to write them.

An Explanation of the Book's Organization

Utilizing all the progress that has been made in the teaching of reading and writing, these literary units affirm and extend what we are now doing in the classroom. Lukens (1999) states that "a genre is a kind or type of literature that has a common set of characteristics" (p. 13). We have included four genres of children's literature in this book: fiction, which covers the study of realistic fiction and mysteries; traditional literature, which discusses pourquoi stories, fables, folktales, beast tales, and cumulative tales; fantasy, which includes modern folktales and fantasy; and nonfiction, which deals with biographies. We have selected these specific genres of children's literature because we believe that with these, students can move comfortably from reading the genre to writing the genre.

We have provided extensive exploration and study of genres in each chapter but have focused on the elements that remain fairly reliable as a method for identifying each genre. These are the basic elements and structures that make mystery reading and writing different from biography reading and writing, and both different from reading and writing folktales. The more one encounters the elements of the different genres, the easier it will be to identify and to understand how authors use these elements to develop their text.

Teaching Realistic Fiction, Chapter One, identifies the differences between fiction and nonfiction. Understanding that the story seems true to life but was created by the author allows students to understand settings, characters, and conflicts. Because realistic fiction stories have been created by an author, this chapter also discusses author's intent and style.

In Chapter Two, Teaching Mysteries, discussion of characters and plot becomes more complex as students learn about the events, the crime, and the motive in the story. Students find that the characters play different roles in mysteries: sleuth, suspect, villain, and victim. These various roles are realized as the plot progresses and the author plants clues and builds suspense.

Chapters Three and Four venture into the make-believe world, exploring traditional literature and the oral tradition of storytelling. We have selected five types of traditional literature, each with a unique narrative organization. Chapter Three, Teaching Traditional Folktales, looks at why these tales were shared orally—to entertain, not instruct. The study of folktales is a study of cultures, but also includes the basic structure of narrative text. Their linear organization makes folktales and beast tales easy to follow because of patterned beginnings and endings, flat characters, and one-dimensional problems. Cumulative tales are organized in a different manner, with each episode building upon the others. The charm of these tales is found in their repetition and rhyme.

Chapter Four, Teaching Pourquoi Stories and Fables, reviews the narrative structure of both types of tales and explains why these tales were told. Pourquoi tales begin with a question and an explanation of a world long ago and end with the reason why our world is no longer the same. Fables begin with a problem, include stereotypic characters, and end with a life lesson or moral; these tales were told to instruct.

Chapter Five, Teaching Modern Folktales, and Chapter Six, Teaching Fantasy, continue our journey through the world of make believe. The study of modern folktales helps students build bridges between traditional literature and fantasy. Modern folktales have the same narrative structure as traditional tales, but fantasy motifs often are introduced. Two types of modern folktales are covered in Chapter Five—the literary folktale and the spin–off. Chapter Six discusses how fantasy stories suspend disbelief using real and make–believe settings, fantasy motifs, round characters, personification, and twisting plot development.

Chapter Seven, Teaching Biographies, moves into nonfiction or expository text. Studying biographies provides students with a safe entry into studying nonfiction because biography authors have used elements of story in their writing. In the biography unit, students will learn about lifelines, chronological order, round and dynamic characters, and authentic settings. Students will also observe how authors of expository text breathe life into their characters by using dialogue, anecdotes, flashbacks, and jackdaws.

Each chapter in this book has three main sections: Background Information for Teachers, Teaching the Genre, and Extension Activities. The first section, Background Information for Teachers was designed to introduce you to the genre and its literary elements. In this section we have provided a bit of the genre's history, types of stories included in the genre, and the stories' specific literary elements.

The second section of each chapter, Teaching the Genre, suggests specific elements you might want to consider teaching your students. (Beginning Intermediate Level refers to students in Grades 3 and 4 and Intermediate Level refers to students in Grades 5 and 6.) How you teach the elements, of course, depends on your students' ability levels and background knowledge.

In read–aloud sessions, you will read the entire story aloud. During the read–aloud session, draw attention to the essential components for discussing the elements inherent in the text, which allows students to gain the vocabulary needed to talk about the genre. When students gain general knowledge about each genre and the vocabulary necessary to share that knowledge, they are ready to interact with you and with their peers in guided reading sessions. Students will discuss both efferent and aesthetic questions, and they will use the techniques you have modeled to organize their growing understanding of each genre. Both the questions and the organizational techniques help students stay actively involved in the reading of the text.

Finally, with their new knowledge of genre elements, students will write their own genre piece independently. Encourage students to plan this piece of writing using outlines that remind them of the genre elements they gained through their reading. Putting this piece of writing into a final form that can be shared with others creates a community of readers and writers. Publishing students' stories can be as simple as students orally sharing their written pieces with classmates, or being given the opportunity to bind the written pieces and add them to the school library, or submitting their stories to a writing contest. In each chapter, we also include assessments to be given after the Small-Group Guided Reading and the Independent Writing Activities. We believe, as Routman (1991) states, that "the goal of evaluation, like the goal of teaching, is to make the learner self-monitoring, self-regulating, and in-dependent" (p. 303). Assessment should be formative, occurring during the unit so students and teachers can monitor learning as it happens.

In the third section of each chapter, Extensions, we suggest ways to encourage students to go beyond the reading and writing of each genre and move into research or the arts. These extension activities emphasize the characteristics of each genre, including story line, char-acters, oral tradition, and authorship, to name a few.

Our three-step approach to each genre scaffolds students' learning so they receive support along the way. Focusing instruction on the reading and writing of the literary genres will not only foster inde-pendent and engaged readers but will also nurture and aid students in gaining control of written discourse. This book presents an interac-tive model that utilizes quality children's literature as the foundation for teaching reading and writing.

Chapter One

Teaching Realistic Fiction

Realistic Fiction is a popular genre among students of all ages. Reading about humorous events, survival escapades, maturing, living with different types of people, and reacting to the "light" and the "dark" sides of life helps us understand ourselves, our relationships with others, and our life experiences.

Background Information for Teachers

Although this unit is designed for Grades 3 through 6, teaching literary elements can be customized for students' varying ability levels and their background knowledge of the genre. The beginning intermediate students (Grades 3 and 4) can study the basic elements of realistic fiction, while intermediate level students (Grades 5 and 6) can learn additional elements that will enhance their reading and writing. (See Figure 1.1 on page 8 for a chart of Elements by Level.)

Definition

The publication of *Robinson Crusoe* (1719) by Daniel Defoe marked the beginning of realistic fiction as a genre of literature. Realistic fiction is a classification of literature that contains stories that could happen in the real world, in a time and a setting that is possible, with characters that are true to life. The central character's problem makes up the plot and is the source of the conflict. Hillman (1999) states that "realistic fiction, then, is the 'real' story; it is what we perceive reality to be, filtered through the literary devices of story" (p. 166). Lukens (1999) states "character and conflict are both well developed and interrelated" (p. 15). Books such as *The Last of the Mohicans* (1826) by James Fenimore Cooper, *Little Women* (1868) by Louisa May Alcott, and *The Adventures of Tom Sawyer* (1876) by Mark Twain also fall within this genre.

Figure 1.1   Elements by Level

Beginning Intermediate	Intermediate

The Story
  Introduction–setting, characters, problem
  Setting–integral
  Characters–round, dynamic
  Conflict–problem
  Plot–types
 	
Author's Style–
  figurative language–similes and metaphors
 	
Theme
	The Story
	  Introduction–prior events, characters (round, dynamic, static, flat, protagonist, antagonist)
	  Setting–integral, backdrop
	  Conflict–problem
	  Plot–types
	  Variations of Plot–foreshadowing and flashbacks
	
	Author's Style–
	  point of view, imagery, figurative language (similes and metaphors), author's intent
	
	Theme

The difference between *historical* realistic fiction and *contemporary* realistic fiction is a matter of time periods. Literary experts usually define contemporary realistic fiction as books published either after World War II or after the 1960s. In this chapter *contemporary* is defined as the period between the 1960s and the present.

Literary Elements of Realistic Fiction

Realistic fiction is structured as a narrative. The introduction includes background information that is needed to understand the story, and establishes the setting, the characters, and the conflict. The middle of the story develops the plot, which includes the story's events, the characters' reactions to these events, and the roadblocks the characters encounter. Usually the plot builds events to a climax, which is called rising action plot development. The story ends with a resolution to the conflict or a conclusion.

It may be helpful to describe the elements of realistic fiction to students using the following basic definitions:

Introduction is where the author builds the story's background. This is where the reader learns about the setting, the characters, and the story's conflict, and perhaps what took place before the story begins.

Setting is where and when the story takes place: location, season, weather, and time period (Tompkins, 1994). Setting is important to the plot, the characters, the characters' problems, and the theme. For example, in realistic fiction the season and the weather may be important to the characters' dilemma. Because realistic fiction must depict characteristics of the real world, authors must develop detailed descriptions of the setting so that the reader can imagine the setting and understand the characters and their plights.

Characterization allows the reader to learn about what characters look like, what they say, what others say about them, and what they do (Lukens, 1999). Characters seem real because their actions and dialogue are believable. As readers, we often can identify with these characters because they are like our friends or ourselves

There are many types of characters in realistic fiction. The main character is usually fully developed and multifaceted and is called a *round character*. If this character changes during the story, this character is also *dynamic*. *Flat characters* are not as well-developed as round characters. *Static characters*, on the other hand, can be round or flat characters who do not change but stay the same in the story. A character who has the opposite personality traits of the main character is called a *foil character*.

Characters can also be classified as a *protagonist* or an *antagonist*. The protagonist is usually the main character who is involved in a conflict. The antagonist is the character who is the opposing force in the conflict.

Conflict in realistic fiction is defined by the type of problem in the story. Conflict is the tension that exists between the forces in the character's life.

Person-against-self is a conflict where the main character is both the protagonist and the antagonist. The character must work out relationships with others, feelings of conflict, and problems. One book that illustrates person-against-self conflict is *On My Honor* (1986) by Marion Dane Bauer. In this book, the main character, Joel, has to resolve the conflict of whether to tell his parents, his friend's parents, and the authorities what happened to his best friend, Tony.

Person-against-person is a conflict that puts the protagonist in direct conflict with another person. One example, *The Pinballs* (1987) by Betsy Byars, contains three characters that meet each other in a foster home and are in conflict with other people. Harvey is in conflict with his father; Carlie is in conflict with her stepfather; and Thomas J. is in conflict with his parents, who abandoned him when he was 2 years old.

Person-against-nature is a conflict where the main character has to fight nature. An example of this type of conflict is *Hatchet* (1987) by Gary Paulsen. In this story, Brian has to survive in the wilderness with only a hatchet, a gift from his mother.

Person-against-society is a conflict where society is the antagonist in a story, and the main character must figure out how to overcome the pressures of the society in which he or she lives. An example of this type of conflict is *Journey to Jo'burg* (1986) by Beverly Naidoo. In this story, Naledi and Tirs must fight the racial adversities placed on them by the white people in South Africa in order to contact their mother and bring her home to care for their ill sister.

Plot is what happens in the story. Cornett (1999) explains that "plot is the sequence of events usually set in motion by a *problem* that begins the action or causes conflict" (p. 89). The plot in realistic fiction must be believable or possible and easily understood, fast-paced and moving toward resolving the conflict. Two types of plots found in realistic fiction are the *progressive* and the *episodic* plots.

Progressive plot is common in realistic fiction. The story begins with one event and all the other events are tied to the same story line. These events form a chain, with each event leading to the next event until the main character resolves the conflict. Examples of realistic fiction books with progressive plots include *Maniac Magee* (1990) by Jerry Spinelli and *Stone Fox* (1980) by John Reynolds Gardiner. (See Figure 1.2 for an example of progressive plot development.)

Episodic plot occurs when the author tells short stories that are related by setting or characters. *Fig Pudding* (1996) by Ralph Fletcher, *Skinnybones* (1982) by Barbara Park, and *Beezus and Ramona* (1990) by Beverly Cleary all contain episodic plots.

Figure 1.2 Progressive Plot

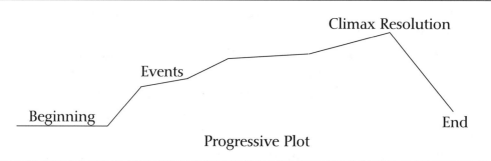

Figure 1.3 Episodic Plot Diagram

Authors use other techniques such as *flashbacks* and *foreshadowing* to vary the plot. Flashbacks allow the author to refer to a period before the actual story being told to fill in the background information for the reader. Foreshadowing allows the author to drop hints about how the main character will solve the problem. (See the example of an episodic plot diagram shown in Figure 1.3.)

Theme, according to Lukens (1999), is "the idea that holds the story together,...the central meaning of a piece of writing" (p. 135). Realistic fiction is often classified according to its themes, which center around the need to be loved, to belong, to achieve, to be secure, or to know. Realizing the theme of a story is a personal response; each reader brings his or her own personal meaning to the story. This personal response is a "life–to–text" connection.

Therefore, what individual students identify as theme may differ. For example, lets look briefly at the story by Marilyn Sachs, *The Bears' House*. In this story, Fran Ellen, a fourth grader, must hide her home situation of living with an ill mother and an absent father, while tending to her brothers and sisters and coping with an unfriendly school situation; Fran Ellen escapes these adversities by playing with her teacher's doll house. Individual student responses might focus on the themes of loving and caring for family members, surviving at school, living without parents, finding relief from adversity, or receiving a gift. Depending on the individual student's perspective and his or her life experiences, the transaction with the text will differ.

Authors use different elements to capture the reader's interest. They use different points of view to tell their story, and they use imagery and figurative language to build pictures in the reader's mind. Authors also write with a certain intent. This intent of the author is how the author wants the reader to feel as the story is read.

Point of view is the perspective of the storyteller. When a story is written from the first-person point of view, the main character usually tells the story and uses the word "I." *Fig Pudding* (1996) by Ralph Fletcher, *The Bears' House* (1996) by Marilyn Sachs, and *Dear Mr. Henshaw* (1996) by Beverly Cleary are written in first person.

When a story is written from the third-person point of view, the person telling the story is a central observer who knows all (omniscient) and can recount details, actions, thoughts, and feelings of the characters (conscious and unconscious). The author writes from a storyteller's perspective and uses pronouns such as "he," "she," and "they." Stories written from this point of view include *On My Honor* (1986) by Marion Dane Bauer, *Journey to Jo'burg* (1986) by Beverly Naidoo, and *The Goats* (1987) by Brock Cole.

Imagery refers to the author's choice of descriptive words and phrases that help readers form a mental picture of settings, characters, and events, thus keeping readers fully involved in the story. The following example of imagery is from Ralph Fletcher's book *Fig Pudding* (1996) in which the author describes how Grandma made stollen for the holidays:

> She gave Josh a pile of walnuts and a block of wood for breaking the nuts into smaller pieces. That was a tradition: whenever Grandma made stollen the youngest kid always got to smash up the walnuts. Josh took the wood and started pounding like a madman, as if he wanted to pulverize each walnut right down to the dust. (p. 18)

Figurative language, including similes and metaphors, is used in realistic fiction to enhance imagery. *Similes* are comparisons that make use of "like" or "as." A *metaphor* compares two unlike things directly without using like or as. This example of a simile is found in *Fig Pudding* where one of the characters describes his grandma: "One time when she fell asleep on the couch I spent fifteen minutes studying her hands, the dark veins slowly throbbing under her skin that looked thin and clear as tissue paper" (p. 17). This description of Grandma continues on, but this time the author uses a metaphor: "Her hands made me think of driftwood, old and pale and worn smooth" (p. 17).

Author's intent or **tone** relates to how the author wants readers to feel as we read the book. An author can intend the story to be humorous, sad, serious, slapstick, or any combination of these throughout the story, and will use sentence structure, word choices, patterns and arrangements to communicate and set the story's tone (Lukens, 1999).

Variety Within the Genre

Because there are a number of themes in realistic fiction, most experts delineate categories of realistic fiction using aspects of theme. Among these categories, themes such as living in a diverse world, accepting differences, living with others, and growing up are all superimposed. This section will focus on five themes that occur often in comtemporary realistic fiction:

Family and friends stories revolve around family matters and relationships with others. Examples of books in this category are *Journey to Jo'burg* (1986) by Beverly Naidoo, *The Bears' House* (1996) by Marilyn Sachs, *Fig Pudding* (1996) by Ralph Fletcher, and *Flip-Flop Girl* (1996) by Katherine Paterson.

Humorous stories revolve around a problem, but depict the funny side of life. Books like *All About Sam* (1990) by Lois Lowry, *Fudge-a-mania* (1990) by Judy Blume, *Sideways Stories From Wayside School* (1985) by Louis Sachar, and *Attaboy, Sam!* (1992) by Lois Lowry all fit into this category.

Survival stories describe how the main character must overcome adverse conditions in order to stay alive. *Hatchet* (1987) by Gary Paulsen, *The Goats* (1987) by Brock Cole, and *My Side of the Mountain* (1988) by Jean Craighead George are all survival stories.

Animal stories feature an animal as the central character of the story. The animals in these stories have realistic traits and are not personified. In these stories, the antagonist can be nature as in *Incredible Journey* (1996) by Shelia Burnford, or other people as in the book *Shiloh* (1991) by Phyllis Reynolds Naylor. Other books in this category are *Where the Red Fern Grows* (1996) by Wilson Rawls and *Stone Fox* (1980) by John Reynolds Gardiner.

Sports stories deal with sports as part of the main theme. These stories deal with perseverance, sportsmanship, and game description. Conflict centers around person–against–self as in the story *The Trading Game* (1990) by Alfred Slote, where the main character tries to sift out the importance of family versus winning. Person–against–society is the theme in Robert Weaver's *Nice Guy, Go Home* (1968), where the main character in a baseball story is Amish. Females are also portrayed in sports stories, as in *Spike It!* (1998) by Matt Christopher. Other books in this category include *Snowboard Showdown* (1999) and *The Fox Steals Home* (1985) by Matt Christopher.

Teaching the Realistic Fiction Story

There are three instructional arrangements used in this unit: a whole-class read-aloud, small-group guided reading, and individual writing of realistic fiction. Each instructional arrangement will be discussed in detail. The first instructional arrangement, whole-class read-aloud, has two components: pre–read-aloud activities and during read-aloud activities.

Pre–Read-Aloud Activities

The pre–read-aloud activities revolve around building background knowledge of the genre, developing an understanding of realistic fiction, and preparing students for reading realistic fiction.

To begin the unit on realistic fiction, conduct a brainstorming session to find out what students already know about realistic fiction. After students have relayed what they know about this genre, discuss the difference between fiction and nonfiction. Tell them that fiction is a type of literature that contains stories that might be possible in the real world, but these stories are made up and did not really happen; nonfiction stories are about things that did occur and include biographies and autobiographies. Explain that in realistic fiction, the characters act like real people, the setting could be a real place, the characters experience problems of real children, and the resolution could happen in the real world, but the stories did not actually happen. To give an example, read from the credit section found in the biography, *The Story of Harriet Tubman: Conductor of the Underground Railroad* (1991) by Kate McMullen, where the author states

> The events described in this book are true. They have been carefully researched and excerpted from authentic autobiographies, writings, and commentaries. No part of this biography has been fictionalized.

Compare this testament to the note in the credit section from the book *Flip-Flop Girl* (1996) by Katherine Paterson:

> No character is this book is intended to represent any actual person; all the incidents of the story are entirely fictional in nature.

These examples will spark a discussion of the differences between fiction and nonfiction. After the concepts of fiction and nonfiction have been introduced, give students a Realistic Fiction Quiz (see Figure 1.4). This quiz includes matching the titles of popular realistic fiction stories to the main characters.

Figure 1.4   Realistic Fiction Quiz

Can you match the main character to the book title?

Main Character	Book Title
1. Jerry	a. *Dogs Don't Tell Jokes*
2. Leslie	b. *Skinnybones*
3. Meg	c. *Dear Mr. Henshaw*
4. Applesauce	d. *Bridge to Terabithia*
5. Sam	e. *The Leaves in October*
6. Gary	f. *My Side of the Mountain*
7. Alex	g. *The War With Grandpa*
8. Pete	h. *The Chocolate War*
9. John	i. *A Summer to Die*
10. Livvy	j. *Aldo Ice Cream*
11. Leigh	k. *Crash*

Answers: 1–h; 2–d; 3–I; 4–j; 5–f; 6–a; 7–b; 8–g; 9–k; 10–e; 11–c.

If students are unable to match the book titles to the characters, invite them to read the books listed in the quiz to find the answers.

Read-Aloud Activities

To develop an understanding of the elements of realistic fiction, you must select a book for a whole–class read–aloud. While reading this story, you will teach, demonstrate and apply the elements of realistic fiction. Have the following charts ready: Circle of Friends Map (page 17), Determining Round Characters Map (page 19), Life Events by Character Chart (page 20), Plot Diagram (page 22), Rising and Falling Plot Chart (page 23), and Author's Style Chart (page 25).

Introduce the read–aloud by telling the book's title and author, then share the entire story by reading it aloud to the class. The book used in this chapter to model the literary elements of realistic fiction is *Flip-Flop Girl* (1996) by Katherine Paterson. This is an appropriate read–aloud for fourth and fifth grades. However, all activities and questions used in this unit are suitable for most realistic fiction stories, so you could read any realistic fiction story to your class. (See the bibliography's realistic fiction section on page 155 for additional book selections.) Share the questions in this section before reading aloud in order to set purposes for listening; allow students to answer the questions and discuss the story once you have finished reading.

Building Background of the Story

Flip-Flop Girl begins with an introduction of what is happening in Vinnie's life when the story begins. The setting is a funeral home, and Vinnie's father has died of cancer. Other background information provided are the characters at the funeral home and the angry dialogue between Vinnie and Mason, her brother.

Evaluating Setting

The setting in realistic fiction is integral to the story, the main character, and the theme. These questions and activities help students understand the importance of a realistic setting to the development of the character or problem:

1. Where does the story take place?
2. Does the weather or the season affect the characters or the plot?
3. Does the author describe the setting using enough detail for you to gain an understanding of how the setting affects the characters?
4. Could the setting that the author developed be a "real" place, existing in our times?

In this story, the setting becomes the major problem for the main character, Vinnie. Vinnie's father has died of cancer, and her mother cannot afford to stay in Washington, so the family must move in with Vinnie's grandmother in Texas.

After the read–aloud is completed, discuss the descriptions of the settings in relation to the main character, the main character's problem, and the events in the plot. This discussion will lead readers to the conclusion that the setting is indeed important to the story line. The setting is the main source of Vinnie's problem: a new town, new school, no friends, and taking care of Mason at school.

Identifying Types of Characters

The questions and activities in this section help students identify four types of characters—round, dynamic, foil, and static—and the relationships of these characters' problems, actions, thoughts, and moods. These questions can be asked about any character in realistic fiction:

1. Who is the protagonist (main character) in this story?
2. Who are the characters that are in the main character's life?
3. Which characters are fully developed? (round characters)
4. Which characters change as the story progresses? (dynamic characters)
5. Does the author develop a character that displays the opposite personality traits of the main character? (foil character)
6. Who is your favorite character in the story? Why?
7. Do you know any people in your life that remind you of any of the characters in this story?

The protagonist in *Flip-Flop Girl* is Vinnie, because she is the main character and the character whose actions move the story along.

A Circle of Friends Map could be designed to illustrate the other people who are part of the story. The Circle of Friends Map clearly illustrates that the people in the story change as the story progresses. Therefore, it might be useful to design two Circle of Friends Maps, one for before the story begins and one for during the story (see Figure 1.5).

In order to identify the round characters in the story, the attributes of the characters presented in the Circle of Friends Maps need to be

Figure 1.5   Circle of Friends Map

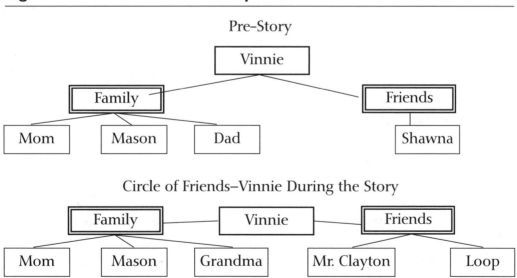

collected and analyzed. For the story *Flip-Flop Girl*, students need to assess the following characters: Vinnie, Mason, Mom, Grandma, Mr. Clayton, and Loop. For example, the attributes of Vinnie might include the following: dislikes Brownsville, likes her teacher, is mean to Mason, picks up Mason after school, eats alone in the cafeteria, plays hopscotch with Loop, dreams, remembers her father, cries, has long hair, wears clothes from the Salvation Army.

Organize character attributes by using the different categories of a round character—what the character looks like, what the character does and thinks, and what others say about the character—on the Determining Round Characters Map (see Figure 1.6). List each character in the story on the chart, and as you collect the attributes of each character, fill in the chart and determine the round characters in the story. By analyzing the attributes, students find two round characters in this story: Vinnie and Loop.

At the end of the story, discuss which characters changed during the story in order to identify the dynamic characters. Develop a Life Events by Character Chart to illustrate events in each character's life and their responses to these events. For example, a Life Events by Character Chart for *Flip-Flop Girl* could be designed for Vinnie and Loop. This chart can be filled in as the story progresses (see Figure 1.7 on page 20).

From the information charted for the two characters, Vinnie and Loop, students will find that Loop displays personality traits opposite those of Vinnie and is a foil character. The author develops a foil to stress the traits of the main character.

Clarifying the Conflict

The problem or conflict in realistic fiction must be possible in life. The following questions help students identify and clarify the types of conflict in the story:

1. What is the conflict in this story?
2. Are the other characters in the story drawn into this conflict by the main character?

Person–against–self is the type of conflict presented in *Flip-Flop Girl*. To document this answer, share the following information as the read-aloud progresses: Throughout the story, Vinnie takes out the anger she feels about her father's death and her move on the other characters in the story. During the first months in her new environment, Vinnie's

Figure 1.6 Determining Round Characters Map

Character	Appearance	Acts	Speech	Thoughts	Others Say
Vinnie	wears brown leather shoes, cotton dress	looks after Mason; plays hopscotch with Loop	"I don't want to pack. I don't want to move." (p. 8)	should she tell mother what she said to Mason? misses her father.	"She's a bit poorly today, but she does hate to miss." (p. 95)
Loop	6 feet tall, wears glasses, stringy black hair, colored skin	plays hopscotch with a stone; picks pumpkins; works in neighbor's yard	"Wanna play?" (p. 8) "You need your own rock." (p. 24)	reads Vinnie's thoughts; likes her real name; believes her father is innocent	"Her father brought her down here last year. From someplace up North—Boston, New York. I forget." (p. 53) "Poor child." (p. 53)
Mason	big, ghostly eyes, toothless grin	makes monkey faces	"Don't cry, Momma," he said. (p. 117)		"He's not noisy...." (p. 26). "We heard your little brother is the worst kid in kindergarten," a girl named Taylor said. (p. 67)
Momma	beautiful; wears Daddy's old plaid jacket; carries big shoulder bag	marches up the stairs at the school	"If you packed your own things, Vinnie–" (p. 8). "Nurses can always get jobs." (p. 8)		

19

Figure 1.7   Life Events by Character Chart—Vinnie and Loop

Event	Reactions of Vinnie	Reactions of Loop
Moves to new city	angry	finds work
Lives with Grandma	unhappy	helps Grandma in pumpkin patch
Loses father	very angry	supports father
No friends	uncomfortable	plays alone
Appearance	embarrassed	comfortable wearing flip-flops

grief and anger are evident in her mean treatment of her silent younger brother, Mason, and her grieving mother and grandmother, as well as her criticism of the only person who befriends her, Loop. She misplaces her grief over the loss of her father on her unsuspecting fourth–grade teacher, and she tries to replace her father's love with that of her teacher.

Following the Plot

The plot is the structure of the story and consists of a series of episodes or events; the plot can be either progressive or episodic. The following questions and activities will help students follow the progression of the plot in a realistic fiction story:

1. How is the plot organized?
2. What are the main events in this story?
3. How exciting are each of these events?
4. What roadblocks did the characters encounter?
5. What is the high point of the story?

The plot for the story *Flip-Flop Girl* is organized using a progressive plot structure. Two graphic organizers can be used to answer the other questions for plot. The first is called a Plot Diagram, which was adapted from one created by Macon, Bewell, and Vogt (1991). To complete the Plot Diagram, students collect the following information during the read–aloud: the title of the story, the main conflict, the events that include the roadblocks or the setbacks of the character and are identified as falling action, the high point of the story, and the solution. A Plot Diagram for the story *Flip-Flop Girl* would look like Figure 1.8 (see page 22).

Another graphic display is the Rising and Falling Plot Chart (see Figure 1.9 on page 23) adapted from the plot profile by Johnson and Louis (1987). To complete this chart, identify the events of the story. Looking at each event in the top portion of the Plot Diagram in Figure 1.8, have students determine the excitement (or the rising action) of each event. Then plot these events on a graph according to whether the intensity of the event was rising or falling. Individual events may also be placed on cards, and students can negotiate the degree of rising or falling actions. Since each reader interprets text from his or her background experiences, these plot maps may differ. Then, using the Plot Diagram from Figure 1.8, plot these events in the Rising and Falling Plot Chart, which might look like the chart in Figure 1.9.

Understanding how the author structures the story will aid in understanding how the events are tied to one another to build the rising and falling action of the story. Explain to students that authors use two literary techniques to vary the plot—flashbacks and foreshadowing. If the author wants to fill in missing information about an event that happened before the story began, the author will use flashbacks; if the author wants to hint at events to come, he or she will use foreshadowing. An example of a flashback from the read–aloud text is:

> She also cut Daddy's hair. Even when he was sick, he would joke with Sheila [her Mom]. The treatments made him nearly bald, but Sheila would trim the few thin strands he had left.
> "It's straight as a stick, Sheila," he'd say.
> "What about a little body wave?" (p. 48)

An example of foreshadowing is found in the text where the Flip–Flop Girl is writing a message to her teacher on the playground. The message said "Congratulations, Mr. C" (p. 51).

Explain that the *climax* of the story is the highest point, the event in which all the actions and responses of the main character come together so that he or she can finally solve the problem or resolve the conflict. The *resolution* is how or what the character does to solve the problem. The actual ending is brief with little detail. Questions to ask about the ending include those that follow on page 23.

Figure 1.8   Plot Diagram

Story: *Flip-Flop Girl*

Problem:	Vinnie is angry about losing her father. She becomes angry at everyone–even those who are nice to her.
Sequence of events:	1. Vinnie moves to her grandmother's house. 2. Vinnie goes to a new school. 3. Vinnie has to go to her new classroom by herself. 4. Loop asks Vinnie to play hopscotch. 5. Loop brings a pumpkin to class. 6. Teacher, Mr. Clayton, gives Vinnie two barrettes. 7. Mason runs away; Vinnie is left to explain to the principal where Mason is; Mr. Clayton saves Vinnie and gives her a ride home. 8. Mr. Clayton gives Loop sneakers. 9. Mr. Clayton gets married. 10. Vinnie scratches teacher's car and lets the blame go to Loop. 11. Mason runs away because Vinnie is mad at him. 12. Flip Flop girl helps save Mason. 13. Vinnie is grateful to Loop and becomes more empathetic to others.
Rising Action (exciting events):	1. Vinnie moves to her grandmother's house. 2. Vinnie goes to a new school. 3. Vinnie has to go to her new classroom by herself. 4. Loop asks Vinnie to play hopscotch. 6. Teacher, Mr. Clayton, gives Vinnie two barrettes. 10. Vinnie scratches teacher's car and lets the blame go to Loop. 11. Mason runs away because Vinnie is mad at him.
Falling Action (roadblocks or setbacks):	5. Loop brings a pumpkin to class. 7. Mason runs away, Vinnie is left to explain to the principal where Mason is; Mr. Clayton saves Vinnie and gives her a ride home. 8. Mr. Clayton gives Loop sneakers. 9. Mr. Clayton gets married. 12. Flip Flop girl helps save Mason. 13. Vinnie is grateful to Loop and becomes more empathetic to others
Climax (highest excitement point):	11. Mason runs away.
Resolution:	13. Vinnie starts to be more empathetic of others.

1. When did the climax take place?
2. What is the story's resolution?
3. How did the story end?
4. Do you have any unanswered questions at the end of the story?
5. Were you pleased with how the story ended?

Identifying the Theme

The theme is the reason authors write stories. Authors write about what they have experienced or know well. Two questions that can be asked about theme are

1. Why do you think the author wrote this story?
2. What was the author's message in this story?

The theme in the story *Flip-Flop Girl* is overcoming grief and be-coming empathetic toward others. To help students better understand the story's theme, discuss grief and the grieving process.

Figure 1.9   Rising and Falling Plot Chart

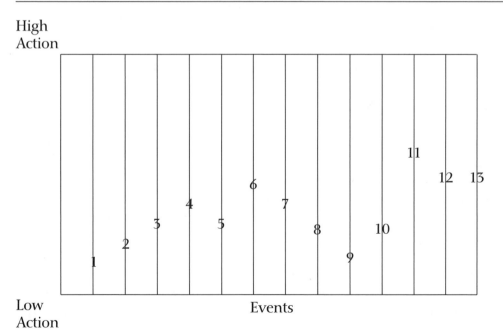

Understanding the Author's Style

To help students understand that authors use different literary techniques to bring their stories to life, introduce point of view, imagery, figurative language, and tone. Use the following activities and questions:

1. Who is telling this story? (point of view)
2. Did the author write in a way that made it easy to visualize the events in the story? (imagery)
3. What literary devices did the author use to capture and maintain your interest in the story? (figurative language)
4. What was the author's intent for writing this story?

Explain that point of view is the vantage point from which the story is told. It refers to the side of the story that the reader will hear. An author can choose to write from four points of view, but only two will be discussed in this unit: first–person and omniscient or third–person point of view. *Flip-Flop Girl* is told from the omniscient point of view.

To answer Questions 2 through 4, ask students to find text examples that illustrate imagery, figurative language, and tone.

Examples of metaphors in *Flip-Flop Girl* are

There was nothing he'd rather be than strange, unless it was a monster from outer space. (p. 26)
The view was something from *The Wizard of Oz*. (p. 41)

Some examples of similes in *Flip-Flop Girl* are

It would be like asking the Wicked Witch of the West if you could play with her flying monkeys. (p. 24)
On the playground, however, with no teachers around, the girl stood out like the golden arches at a McDonald's. (pp. 20–21)
Her hair was as long and stringy as Vinnie's, but it was black as Monna's funeral outfit. (p. 21)

The author intended to write this story with a serious tone. To document the various literary elements that authors use to convey tone, have students collect examples on the Author's Style Chart (see Figure 1.10).

To bring it all together, after studying literary elements of realistic fiction with the class, one sixth–grade teacher asked her students to come up with their own definitions for the elements:

Setting: some place where the story takes place in the book

Characters: the most important part of the story; if there were no characters in the story, there would be no story; the story is based on the characters

Solution: characters try to solve a problem or try to live with it

Conflict: a problem that the character deals with a lot

Theme: the message or lesson learned from the book

Author's Intent: what the book was like—serious, funny, scary, sad, or surprising

Point of View: first–person or third–person; depends on who is telling the story

Figure 1.10   Author's Style Chart

Book _____

Theme _____

Point of View _____

Examples of Similes (use like or as) _____

_____

Examples of Metaphors (do not use like or as) _____

_____

Examples of Imagery (great description) _____

_____

Author's Intent _____

_____

Small-Group Guided Reading

Now give students the opportunity to read and explore other realistic fiction stories. The questions and instructional activities shared during the read–aloud can be used during the small–group guided reading of realistic fiction. At this time, you and your students should plan the mapping strategies and questions that they will use while reading their book. The questions and the mapping activities are general enough to use with any piece of realistic fiction. Because students have worked through the questions and the strategies with you as the model, they should feel comfortable using them in small groups. You and the students might decide what strategies to repeat, and students should feel comfortable adding some of their own questions to bring to the discussion table. Students can use any of the maps, charts, and outlines in this chapter to answer questions about the story.

Questions for Small-Group Guided Reading

1. How did your group decide on which questions and activities to use? Were your questions and activities effective in helping you understand realistic fiction?
2. From the book you read, identify and describe a dynamic character, a foil character, or a static character.
3. Discuss the problem in the book and describe the type of conflict.
4. Give an example of how the author uses foreshadowing or flashbacks to keep your interest in the story.
5. Identify the author's intent for telling this story and give the reasons for your answer.

Independent Writing of Realistic Fiction

An effective way to help students see the whole picture of the literary components used in realistic fiction is to write a story themselves. This independent writing of realistic fiction will follow the writing process: prewriting, drafting, revising, editing, and publishing.

As students plan the writing of their own realistic fiction, an outline may prove helpful. This outline allows students to decide on the problem, create the list of characters, and plot the entire story line before they begin their first draft. Students may complete this outline from beginning to end. In the prewriting stage, ask students to create a Realistic Fiction Map (see Figure 1.11) and choose strategies to flesh out their outline.

Now students can begin to fill in their outline by using the techniques that were modeled and practiced in the read–aloud and applied in small–group guided reading. Students may wish to use the Determining Round Character Map, the Circle of Friends Map, and the Life Events by Character Chart to describe the main character and the other characters. To organize the events, students might design a Plot Diagram or a Rising and Falling Plot Chart identifying the story's events, the roadblocks, and rising action.

Figure 1.11   Realistic Fiction Map

1. Decide why you are telling this story. (author's intent/tone)
2. Decide on the problem or the conflict. (problem)
3. Decide who will tell the story. (point of view)
4. Where will your story take place? (setting)
5. Decide on the characters. (characterization)
    a. the protagonist–round character, dynamic
    b. the antagonist
    c. two flat characters

Main Characters
6. Design a Round Character Map of at least one character, illustrating the attributes of this character.
7. Design a Circle of Friends Map for this main character.
8. Decide how this character will change.
9. Decide on at least three events in the story.

Plot
10. Decide on the last event, the event that will be the climax.
11. Decide how the main character will solve the problem or resolve the conflict.
12. Decide how you will end the story.
13. Design the outline of the story:
    a. *Beginning:* How will you introduce the story using background information, the setting, the characters, and the protagonist's problem.
    b. *Middle:*   List the events that you will put in the story, including three events, the main character's responses, and the other characters' responses.
    c. *End:*   How will the story end?

Leah wrote this piece of realistic fiction when this unit was taught in a fifth-grade classroom. When asked how she came up with the topic for her piece, she said that she wanted to write a story about the woods.

The Evening Walk
by Leah

It's a snowy night when Mom slips on her boots. The house is dark but I can see. She walks out onto the porch. I follow silently.

We walk across the snow trying not to sink in. Our shadows follow us like a baby chick and a hen. The trees stir as we walk. A rabbit scampers to the right. All I hear is our feet crunching on the ice-covered snow. My Mom pauses, inhaling the pine-scented air. I see fox tracks going east. My Mom points at a clearing. There is a fawn and its mother. We watch them. They watch us. All is silent. I move, stepping on a branch. Crack! They sprint off into the darkness. We are alone once more. A sudden breeze makes me shiver. I breathe deeply watching my breath curl up into the air and disappear. We walk home. The tree branches hang lowly over us. The snow weighs them down. We trudge along. The moon gleams off our rosy cheeks. We reach the house once again.

We are both tired. I slip out of my boots and jacket. I take off my damp snow pants and climb into bed. My Mother kisses my forehead and turns off the light. She whispers in my ear "Good night."

When this unit was taught at the fourth grade level, Chris wrote this story:

Chris the Fisherman
by Chris

Chris the Fisherman was in the middle of Otter Lake. He had been fishing for a very long time. Chris was in a contest to catch the biggest fish. He had been dreaming of this trophy since he was 5 years old.

He was waiting and waiting for the biggest fish in Otter Lake. Suddenly a fish was on his hook. It was the biggest fish Chris had ever seen. Chris and the fish fought for an hour, reeling and tugging. It was a sturgeon! Then it took Chris 5 minutes to get the hook out of the fish's mouth. Chris put the fish on the bottom of the boat because it was too big for the cooler.

Chris went to shore and showed the sturgeon to the judges. He won! He was so excited. It was his first trophy ever. Chris took the fish home in a big, big bucket and had a big, big dinner.

Questions for Independent Writing

This assessment gives the student an opportunity to reflect on the progress of writing realistic fiction. The questions ask students to provide a rationale for their choice of characters, setting, point of view, and also their intent for writing the story.

1. What types of characters did you include in your story? (foil, static, round, dynamic)
2. Describe why you chose your setting and its effect on your character's development or problems.
3. Discuss your intent for writing this story.
4. Whose point of view did you use to tell the story? Why did you decide on this point of view?
5. Would you like to share your realistic fiction with others?
6. Will you write another realistic fiction story?

Realistic Fiction Extensions

To extend this unit, invite students to explore sequels and trilogies. Sometimes readers want to know more about a character and what happened to him or her after the original story ended. Some good examples of these types of books follow:

Sequels:
George, J.C. (1988), *My Side of the Mountain*. New York: Dutton.
George, J.C. (1990). *On the Far Side of the Mountain*. New York: Viking.
Paulsen, G. (1987). *Hatchet*. New York: Viking.
Paulsen, G. (1991). *The River*. New York: Delacorte.

Trilogies:
Naylor, P.R. (1991). *Shiloh*. New York: Dell.
Naylor, P.R. (1996). *Shiloh Season*. New York: Simon & Schuster.
Naylor, P.R. (1997). *Saving Shiloh*. New York: Simon & Schuster.

If there is not a sequel already published, perhaps students would like to write one for their favorite realistic fiction story.

To extend the lesson using drama, invite students to pantomime one event from the story while the other students guess the essence of the pantomime. Closely related to pantomime is Mime Theatre, in which students mime an event in the story while the event is read aloud by one of the students.

Have students write a Clerihew for the main character in the book that they are reading. This type of poetry was named after E. Clerihew Bentley, an English writer during World War II who often included these short rhymes in his columns.

Line 1:   Person's name is at the end of the line
Line 2:   Rhymes with the name in line 1.
Lines 3 & 4: Rhyme with each other.

An example might be

The ambition of Jess
Is to run, not play chess.
But Leslie has something else planned:
A kingdom in another land.

Summary

This realistic fiction unit focused on building an understanding of the important literary elements common to most fictional stories. We identified the differences between nonfiction and fiction and covered the importance of building background knowledge of the story, creating an integral setting, developing types of characters (round, flat, dynamic, static, and foil), and identifying the story's conflict. This unit discussed use of point of view, figurative language, and tone to convey author's intent.

Realistic fiction is our first unit because this genre contains the basic elements of narrative story structure and leads easily into the subgenre of mysteries.

Chapter Two

Teaching Mysteries

A subgenre of realistic fiction, the mystery is a popular genre among adults as well as students because of its characters, scare factor, suspense, and quick-paced action. Mysteries promote active participation by encouraging the reader to make sense of the clues provided.

Background Information for Teachers

This unit is intended for Grades 3 through 6 and can be customized for each grade level dependent upon the ability levels of the students and their background in this genre. Beginning intermediate students (Grades 3 and 4) can study the basic elements of a mystery. Intermediate students (Grades 5 and 6) can learn about additional elements that will improve their reading and mystery writing. (See Figure 2.1 for a breakdown of story elements by level.)

Figure 2.1 Elements by Level

Beginning Intermediate	Intermediate
Setting—backdrop, integral	Setting—backdrop, integral
Characters—round, flat, roles	Characters—round, flat, roles
Plot Development—events, crime, actions, clues	Plot Development—events, progression of crime, actions, clues
Resolution of Crime, Motive, Ending	Suspense—foreshadowing, red herrings, cliffhangers
	Climax, Resolution of Crime, Motive, Ending

Definition

The fundamental characteristic of mysteries, according to Cavelti (1976), is hidden secrets and an investigation. Although mystery stories follow the narrative story structure, including characters, setting, problem, actions, resolution, and ending, the main element of a mystery is suspense. Suspense builds as the reader wonders if and when the mystery will be solved, and questions abound in the mystery story: "who did it?" "what happened?" and "why?"

The intriguing problem and the well-rounded characters' quest to solve the mystery are a big part of this genre's appeal. Huck, Helper, Hickman, and Kiefer (1997) state that students "enjoy the order of a mystery's universe, where loose ends are tied up, everything is explained, and evil is punished" (p. 501).

Literary Elements of Mysteries

A mystery follows the narrative structure where the beginning includes the setting, the characters, and the problem. Within the mystery, the setting is either integral to the plot or a simple backdrop to the action. The main characters are round and fully developed, and the supporting characters are flat. The plot of the mystery is complex and includes the events, the clues to solve the mystery, and the actions of the characters.

Discussing setting depends on the type of mystery that you wish to share with the students. For example, an historical mystery needs to be set in the appropriate time and place. Whether the mystery takes place in a foreign country or in your hometown, that place or location must be researched because the settings are integral to the story. However, if the mystery takes place in a school or office or airport (a backdrop setting), the setting may not be that important to the mystery.

Since the mystery is a subgenre of realistic fiction, the characters must behave like real people. The main characters in the mystery story are fully developed and well-rounded. Lukens (1999) defines a *round character* as one that the author creates by including for the reader the character's appearance, actions, speech, opinions, and what others say and think of this character. Supporting characters are not as fully developed and are referred to as *flat characters*. In mysteries, characters play different types of roles: the *sleuth* is the detective and is usually the main character or the protagonist; the *villain*, or the antagonist, is the character who is the main doer of evil deeds; the *suspects* are those who also are thought to be the villain; and the *victim* is the one who receives the brunt of the evil deeds.

The conflict in a mystery is a crime, a puzzle, or a secret. Plot development, according to Howe (1990), "is the most crucial ingredient in any mystery" (p. 178). Plot revolves around events into which the author sprinkles clues, and plot includes the actions of the characters in response to the clues. Clues can be fingerprints, letters, notes, or secret codes; clues can be discovered by listening carefully to the other characters' dialogue or watching the other characters' actions carefully.

The mystery author's style must create suspense, using any combination of three devices: foreshadowing, red herrings, and cliffhanger chapter endings. *Foreshadowing* is the inclusion of clues throughout the story to provide the reader with information that will lead to the solution of the mystery. *Red herrings* are clues that are placed in the mystery to throw the reader off track and lead the reader away from the mystery's solution. *Cliffhanger chapter endings* use great suspense to compel the reader to read further into the story.

The ending of a mystery contains the climax, the motive, the resolution, and the conclusion of the mystery. The climax involves the interaction between the sleuth and the villain. The motive is what causes the characters to act. The resolution explains how the mystery was solved, and the story's conclusion is brief.

Variety Within the Genre

Within the mystery genre, there are different categories in which mysteries can be placed.

Historical mystery transports readers to a time and place in the past. An example of an historical mystery story for intermediate students is *The Midnight Horse* (1991) by Sid Fleischman. In this story, Jonah, an orphan in 18th-century England, travels to meet his great-uncle, Judge Wigglesford, who turns out to be evil. Jonah, with the help of a ghost magician, must defeat his evil great-uncle. Another story, *Hester Bidgood, Investigatrix of Evil Deeds* (1995) by E.W. Hildick, takes place in Puritan times, where Goody's kitten is found nearly dead and branded. As the story progresses, Goody is declared a witch. The reader must uncover who is responsible for these evil doings.

Detective mystery is a new and upcoming type of mystery for young readers. Traditionally for adults, the private-eye mystery has a detective, clues, an investigation, a solution where the guilty are punished, and all ends well. Examples of mysteries for intermediate students include *The Dead Man in Indian Creek* (1991) by Mary Downing Hahn and Eve Bunting's *Coffin on a Case* (1992).

Laughter and suspense are the incentive for reading **humorous mysteries**. Authors use exaggeration, humorous characters, and funny situations to add humor to a mystery. Examples in this category include Betsy Byars' *Wanted...Mud Blossom* (1993), where other characters play tricks on Junior as he searches for the missing school hamster. In the story *Peppermints in the Parlor* (1993) by Barbara Brooks Wallace, the sarcastic language and the situations involving Emily and her new friend at the retirement home provide humor in the midst of the mystery.

Fantasy mysteries incorporate the world of make-believe by using magic and ghosts to take the reader out of the real world and into the fantasy world. Examples in this category are *The House of Dies Drear* (1968) by Virginia Hamilton and *The Widow's Broom* (1992) by Chris Van Allsburg.

Problem and puzzle mysteries present a problem or puzzle and challenge the reader to solve the problem or the puzzle by following the clues. Usually, a problem is presented in the first chapters, and the story winds the reader through a puzzling sequence of events until the solution to the problem is revealed. This mystery seems to be the most popular type for intermediate readers. Examples of problem and puzzle mysteries are *The Westing Game* (1992) by Ellen Raskin, *The Tormentors* (1990) by Lynn Hall, *The Tangled Webb* (1993) by Eloise McGraw, *Megan's Island* (1990) by Willo Davis Roberts, and *Finding Buck McHenry* (1991) by Alfred Slote.

Teaching the Mystery Story

As in the previous chapter, there are three instructional arrangements used in this unit: a whole class read-aloud, small-group guided reading, and individual writing of a mystery. Each instructional arrangement will be discussed in detail. The first instructional arrangement, whole class read-aloud, has two components: pre-read-aloud activities and during read-aloud activities.

Pre–Read-Aloud Activities

To begin the unit on mysteries, conduct a brainstorming session to determine what students already know about this genre. Record the results of this brainstorming session on a chart in the classroom, then as students become more familiar with the mystery genre, revise and update this chart. You also may want to lead a discussion about students' favorite mysteries.

After the brainstorming session is completed, put humorous definitions of terms associated with mysteries on sentence strips (see Figure 2.2), and ask the students if they can fix these sentences. If they cannot, post these strips in the classroom for the students to ponder and revise as you teach this unit.

To develop students' understanding of the elements of mysteries, choose a book to read aloud to the whole class. While reading this mystery, demonstrate and apply the elements with teaching strategies and by using the following charts, all of which can be found in this chapter: Life Space Map (page 37), Integral Setting Map (page 37), Round Character Map (page 39), Character Sociogram (page 40), and the Mystery Plot Map (page 42). While students are listening to the mystery, ask them to collect information to place on these charts. The number of chapters that you share in one session should depend on your students' attention spans and your class schedule.

Figure 2.2   Preview of Mystery Terms

1. A red herring is *a brightly colored fish.*
2. A victim is *one who finds the clues.*
3. A suspect is *a person who sells suspenders.*
4. Suspense is *the person who wears the suspenders.*
5. A sleuth is *a sailboat.*
6. Foreshadowing is *when a shadow appears just before dark.*
7. A cliffhanger *is a vehicle for hang gliding.*
8. A mystery's plot is *a piece of land where the victim is buried.*

Answers: 1. A red herring is a clue to throw the reader off the real solution. 2. A victim is the one who is affected by the crime. 3. A suspect is a person who is thought to be guilty. 4. Suspense is when the author makes you feel anxiously uncertain about the story's outcome. 5. A sleuth is a detective or the person solving the mystery. 6. Foreshadowing is when clues are slipped in throughout the plot that hint at the outcome. 7. A cliffhanger is when the author creates suspense at the end of a chapter to keep you reading. 8. A mystery's plot is the events and actions of the characters in response to clues presented.

Introduce the mystery that you will share by reading the title and the author's name. The mystery modeled in this unit is *Is Anybody There?* (1990) by Eve Bunting. It is an appropriate read–aloud for fifth and sixth grades, but all activities and questions used in this unit are suitable for most mysteries, so you may choose any book you know well that is appropriate for your grade level. (See page 158 of the bibliography for additional mystery possibilities.)

Read-Aloud Activities

Help students develop a deeper understanding of the elements of mysteries by modeling the narrative structure and the development of suspense during the read–aloud. The charts, maps, and questions provided in this section will give students a visual representation of the elements.

Evaluating Settings

The following questions and activities help students understand that the setting, whether backdrop or integral, is tied to the actions of the characters. These basic questions about setting can be used for any mystery:

1. Where does the story take place? What is the season, time of day, and weather?
2. If the mystery has more than one setting, what are they?
3. Does the author use enough detail to describe the setting so the reader can gain a clear picture of the setting?
4. Is the setting important to solving the mystery? (integral)

When a story has more than one setting, as does *Is Anybody There?*, a Life Space Map will show how the main character's life can be influenced by more than one setting. The Life Space Map of Marcus, one of the main characters, is shown in Figure 2.3.

Collect a list of descriptions for each integral setting during the read–aloud. For example, the integral setting of the Mullens' house in our read–aloud can be seen in the following descriptions:

Setting: The Mullens' House—
lemonade, peanut butter, cookies
dark, mysterious, sunlight, shadows in attic, tidy
creaky, calm, quiet, sounds in bathroom
weird, safe, secure

Figure 2.3   Life Space Map

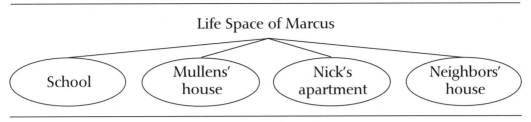

Life Space of Marcus

School   Mullens' house   Nick's apartment   Neighbors' house

Figure 2.4   Integral Setting Map

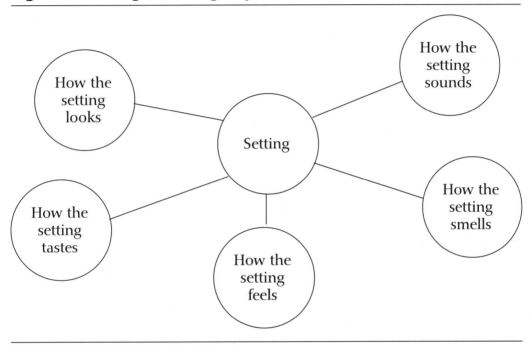

How the setting looks

How the setting sounds

Setting

How the setting tastes

How the setting smells

How the setting feels

Each integral setting can be organized by using an Integral Setting Map like the one shown in Figure 2.4 (adapted from Tompkins, 1994).

Another strategy that can be used to teach integral settings is to have students illustrate the setting using the author's descriptions. Figure 2.5 is an example of a drawing of the setting of the Mullens' house from the reader's mind for the story *Is Anybody There?*

Have students illustrate each setting and add the events of the mystery to the illustration to point out that this setting is integral to solv–

Figure 2.5 Drawing of an Integral Setting

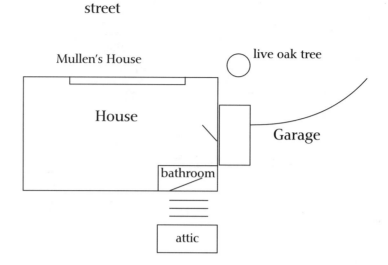

ing the mystery. From the illustration in Figure 2.5, we can visualize where the key was hidden and the layout of the house, the garage, and the attic.

Identifying Types of Characters

Characters in mysteries are either round and well–developed or flat and secondary. The questions in this section help students identify the types of characters, both round and flat, and the roles that these characters play in mysteries. Ask students to name the attributes of characters during the read–aloud and then organize them through the Round Character Map and the Character Sociogram. Basic questions posed to discuss fully developed characters might include:

1. What does the character look like? (appearance)
2. What does the character like to do? (actions)
3. What do others say about the character?
4. What does this character think about?
5. What are the relationships of this character to the other characters in the mystery?

6. What roles do the characters play in mysteries?

Students' answers to the first four questions can be organized on a Round Character Map. In the mystery *Is Anybody There?* the characters are Marcus, his mom, the neighbors, and Nick. Nick is a round character and is described as:

Character: Nick
yellow hair, hair on arms and head, twinkly eyes, large hands and feet, like a big golden bear, wears khaki shorts and t–shirt (appearance)
coaches football, lives in an apartment, cuts grass, teaches physical education (actions)
healthiest person, fittest person, likes butterscotch (what others say)

After the attributes are collected, the class constructs a Round Character Map (adapted from Tompkins, 1994) as shown in Figure 2.6.

Figure 2.6   Round Character Map

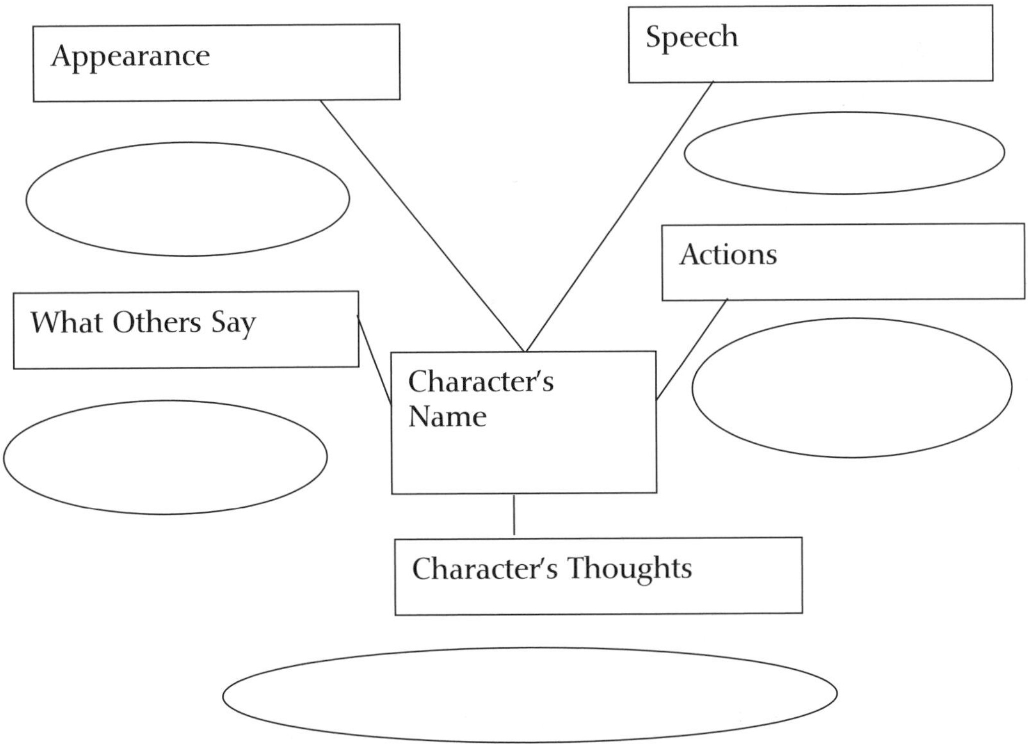

To illustrate, what other characters are in the main character's life and what their relationships are to the main character, the class can develop a Character Sociogram (adapted from Johnson & Louis, 1987). In Figure 2.7, you'll see one example of a character sociogram that was designed for the book, *Is Anybody There?* Figure 2.8 can be given to students to help them work out the relationships of the characters in the read–aloud you are sharing.

Discuss the roles of sleuth or detective, suspects, villain, and victim that characters play in a mystery story. Explain that the sleuth or detective is usually the main character in the story, the character who attempts to solve the mystery by gathering the information, pondering the alternatives, and finally solving the mystery. For example, in *Is Anybody There?*, the sleuth is Marcus Mullen. Suspects are those characters that are thought to be the wrong–doer, the villain, or the one who must be brought to justice and punished. In *Is Anybody There?*, Nick is the suspect. The villain is the one who caused the problem or mystery and sometimes he or she must be brought to justice and punished. Blake is the villain in *Is Anybody There?*, but he is reunited with his father and is not punished. The victim is the character who was wronged. Two victims in *Is Anybody There?* are Marcus and his mother.

Figure 2.7 Character Sociogram

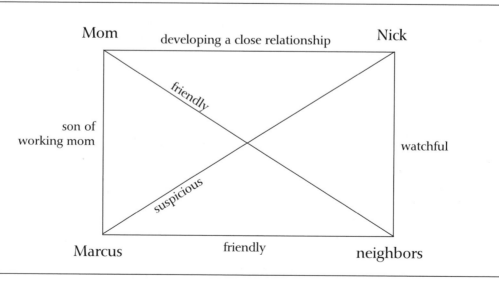

Figure 2.8   Character Sociogram

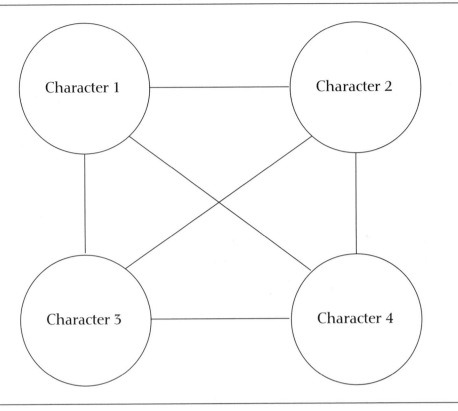

Following the Plot

The plot contains the actions of the characters in response to the crime in the mystery. The questions and activities below help students follow the plot through the sequence of events, the crime, and the responses of the main character. A quick review of the following terms might be helpful to students:

- Events—the situations or episodes in the story
- Progression of the criminal acts—the suspect's opportunities to commit a crime
- Crime—can be a secret that needs to be uncovered, a wrongdoing against another person or thing, or a puzzle to solve
- Actions—how the main character or sleuth responds to the crime; usually the sleuth is responsible for identifying the clues that are significant to the mystery's solution

Use the following questions to help students understand the development of the plot in any mystery:

? 1. What is the problem, crime, or puzzle in the mystery?
2. For each event in the mystery, does the author present a clue and a response of the main character to solve the mystery?

Tell students that in a mystery story, the problem is usually identified in the first chapter. It can be a crime, a puzzle, or a secret. Sometimes, authors include the problem in the title of the book. After you have read the first chapter of your read–aloud, ask students to identify the problem or the mystery, or to predict what the problem or mystery might be. The problem in *Is Anybody There?* is that someone is stealing items from Marcus' house.

Students can use the Mystery Plot Map (see Figure 2.9) to reconstruct the crime by identifying the events in the mystery, the progression of the crime, and the response of the main character to these events.

Figure 2.9   Mystery Plot Map

Reconstruction of Crime

Event 1	Crime	Actions of main character in response to crime
_____	_____	_____
_____	_____	_____
_____	_____	_____

Event 2	Crime	Actions of main character in response to crime
_____	_____	_____
_____	_____	_____
_____	_____	_____

The Mystery Plot Map should be added to continually and completed by the end of the read–aloud.

You could also discuss these additional questions while using the Plot Map.

> 3. Can you predict who the criminal is and the motive for the crime?
> 4. Can you predict the outcome of the mystery?

Allow students to guess at the crime, puzzle, or secret, as long as they give reasons for their guesses.

Explain that the climax is where the detective and the villain collide, and the answer to the conflict is discovered for the first time. In the resolution, all loose ends are tied together: we find out which clues lead to the conflict's resolution; we learn how the villain was identified; we also learn the villain's motive and opportunity for causing the problem or crime.

The actual ending of the story is brief. In the ending, the author ties up all loose details once the solution to the mystery is revealed: What happens to the protagonist or detective? What happens to the suspects, especially the wrong–doer? All questions should be answered in the ending.

Questions that could be posed when discussing the ending might include the following:

> 5. How did the resolution make you feel?
> 6. If you were the author, would you have ended the story in a different way?
> 7. Did you have any unanswered questions at the end of the story?

Understanding the Author's Style

The questions and activities in this section aim to help students understand the author's craft of building suspense and dispensing clues throughout the mystery.

> 1. Can you identify the clues that led you to the solution of the mystery?
> 2. How did the author maintain the suspense throughout the story?

Explain that a *cliffhanger* is a type of suspense that is used at the end of a chapter so that the reader wants to keep reading more. Lukens (1999) states that "the cliffhanger chapter ends with such suspense that a listening child's plea 'Please, just one more chapter!' is irresistible" (p. 117). The cliffhanger chapter endings for *Is Anybody There?* include

> Chapter One:
> I went around the back, dropped my blue nylon book bag by the live oak tree and ducked under for my key. It's dim in there and you can barely see, but my hand knows its way. I felt for the little nub and found it. Then I pushed aside leaves and twigs, peering at the trunk. The nub was empty. The key was gone. (p. 10)

> Chapter Four:
> "Don't worry. The key's safe in here. And the house is locked up tightly. No one could possibly get in."
> But I was wrong about that. (p. 38)

Plan to finish the read–aloud session with a cliffhanger chapter ending, leaving the students begging for one more chapter. Use the opportunity to introduce the cliffhanger and discuss why authors use this type of ending.

Authors use *foreshadowing* to slip clues in throughout the plot that hint at the outcome. These clues lead the reader to the outcome or the solution of the mystery. Foreshadowing in the story *Is Anybody There?* appears when Marcus suspects that Nick, the tenant, is the one invading the privacy of their home. Throughout the story, we find out about Nick from other characters. Miss Sarah, the Mullens' neighbor, brings Christmas cookies over and suggests that Marcus and his mother share them with Nick. In this dialogue between Marcus and Miss Sarah, we discover things about Nick's past:

> Miss Sarah sniffed. "I understand he was married, once."
> "That's what he said."
> "He had a child, too." (p. 28)

In another conversation about Nick, Marcus finds out that Nick does not like peanut butter:

> The Grandma's Bake Shop lady asked which kind [of cookies] we wanted, peanut butter or butterscotch.
> "Butterscotch," Mom said. "He doesn't like peanut butter." (p. 70)

Alert students to the idea of planting clues that will lead the reader to the right conclusion. Point out that all along Marcus thought that Nick was the one entering their home without permission, but when we read the clues and find out about Nick's past and his likes and dislikes, we ask, was it really Nick?

A *red herring* is a clue that is included by the author to mislead the reader, but has no value in actually solving the mystery. (Red herrings are actually small fish that were dragged across a trail to distract tracking hounds.) In *Is Anybody There?* Marcus suspects Nick because he knows that Nick cuts the grass at the Mullens' house. When Marcus finds clumps of grass in the bathroom, he suspects that Nick is the one entering the house.

Small-Group Guided Reading

Now give students the opportunity to read and explore other mysteries. Use the questions and instructional activities shared during the read-aloud during the small-group guided reading of mystery stories.

Give students the opportunity to select a mystery story to read in small groups. (Many of the mysteries found in this book's bibliography are either Edgar Allen Poe Award winners or have been nominated for this award by The Mystery Writers of America.) The questions and mapping strategies modeled in the read-aloud session are general enough to be used for most mysteries. Students have worked through the questions and strategies with you as the model, so now they should feel comfortable using them in small groups. You and the students might decide what strategies to repeat, and students should feel comfortable adding some of their own questions for discussion.

Using the instructional activities presented in the group read-aloud, during small-group reading activities students can identify settings using their choice of an Integral or Life Space Map; identify characters using their choice of a Round Character Map or Sociogram; identify the problem and reconstruct the plot using a Plot Diagram or the Rising and Falling Plot Chart; and identify the climax, resolution, motive and ending. These activities will help them answer questions about their mystery. During this time, encourage students to devise additional questions they are interested in pursuing and to fill in charts that may prove helpful in understanding the mystery they chose to read.

Questions for Small-Group Guided Reading

Have students answer these questions in their guided-reading groups.

1. How did your group decide which questions and activities you would use? Were your questions and activities effective in helping you understand mysteries?
2. Map the settings in the mystery, and tell why each setting was either integral or backdrop to the mystery.
3. What characters were in your mystery? Were these characters round or flat? What roles did these characters play?
4. Map the events as they occurred in the story.
5. What was the motive for the crime?
6. Explain how the author kept you in suspense.

Figure 2.10   Mapping a Mystery

1. Decide on a crime and who did it.

2. Decide on at least four characters:
   a. the victim
   b. the detective
   c. the villain
   d. another suspect

3. Main Characters
   Design a Round Character Map of at least one character, illustrating this character's attributes.
   Design a Character Sociogram indicating the main character's relationships with others.

4. Decide on the motive (the reason behind the crime).

5. Decide how you will announce the villain and how the mystery will end.

6. Design the outline of the mystery:
   Beginning: choose the characters, setting (time and place), and problem to solve.
   Middle: list the events of the crime, the clues, and the character's responses to these events; the most important clues should appear last.
   End: ensure that clues lead to the villain's identification, the motive, and the opportunity.

Independent Writing of Mystery Stories

To help students understand the entire literary structure of mysteries, have them write a mystery themselves. Independently writing mysteries will follow the writing process of prewriting, drafting, revising, editing, and publishing.

As students plan the writing of their own mystery stories, an outline may prove helpful. This allows students to create a cast of characters and the entire story line before they begin their first draft. Students may complete this outline from beginning to end, or they may write out the ending, then work their way back to the beginning of the outline. Figure 2.10 shows an example of the Mapping a Mystery format.

When this unit was taught in his sixth-grade classroom, Lucas seemed to enjoy the writing process and was very organized and methodical. He mapped out his mystery using the Mapping a Mystery format, in which he included a Round Character Map and a Character Sociogram.

Mystery Map by Lucas
_____

1. Crime was: Drive-by shooting and it was done by Jeff Pape.
2. Four characters:
   Victim: Dr. Black Jack
   The Detective: Dr. Joe Shmo
   The Villain: Jeff Pape
   Another Suspect: Johnny Badluck

Round Character Map of Joe Shmo

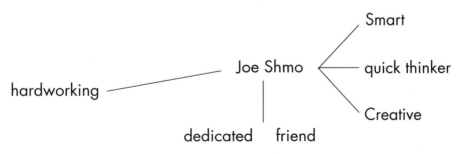

(continued)

Sociogram of Dr. Black Jack

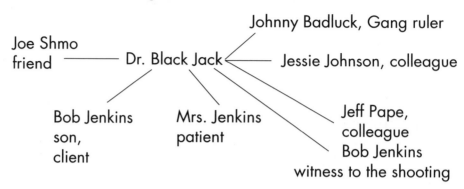

3. Reason for the crime was to make Jeff Pape's dad love him and show him attention.
4. Clues: The death of Mrs. Jenkins
        The drive-by shooting
        Dr. Black Jack's death
        Dr. Joe Shmo going undercover
        Joe Shmo meeting Jeff Pape
        Joe Shmo investigating all the suspects
        Joe Shmo seeing Bob Jenkins leaving Jeff Pape's apartment
        Joe Shmo going to the court house
5. Get everyone together to eliminate each suspect.
6. Outline of the mystery
    Beginning:
    Characters
        Dr. Black Jack
        Dr. Joe Shmo
        Johnny Badluck
        Jessie Johnson
        Jeff Pape
        Bob Jenkins
        Mrs. Jenkins
    Late Night in Chicago on the wrong side of town
    Middle:
    The actual shooting, the color of the car (purple), the kind of car (Lamborghini).
    Johnny Badluck, a gang member and Dr. Black Jack couldn't save his brother in a gang shooting.

48

Bob Jenkins had motive because his mother died under an experimental treatment by Dr. Black Jack.

Jessie Johnson got fired from her job because of Dr. Black Jack.

Bob Jenkins coming out of Jeff Pape's apartment and Jeff was a witness to the actual shooting.

End:

Visit with Jessie Johnson

Records stating Johnny Badluck was no longer in a gang

The green paint that Jeff said he saw on the purple car

Where he was standing in the alley and the side of the car the green paint was on

The fact that he knew Bob Jenkins

The problems that he had with his father

Access to weapons

Students may wish to list and prioritize their clues before drafting. Clues of less significance should be listed first. The last clue should not solve the mystery on its own, but when all clues are put together it should be the one that points to the villain. If students have discussed and want to try their hand at writing red herrings, encourage them to include some to throw the reader off the real solution.

Drafting, Revising, Editing, and Publishing

Now students are ready to complete their first draft. If students wish to get feedback from their peers after writing the first draft, allow them to continue writing and revising their work. When they are pleased with their mystery, you and the other students may help with the editing until the drafts are ready to be published.

After Lucas finished prewriting his mystery, he went through the process and developed his published piece:

Shmo's Investigation
by Lucas

Five years before Dr. Black Jack was killed, he was working on an experimental treatment. Dr. Jack found someone to try his experiment. He convinced a nice elderly woman and her son to try it. Her son gave the permission to go ahead and try the treatment. On a cold winter night late in December, they began the treatment. Suddenly in the middle of the treatment, something went wrong.

Mrs. Jenkins began to have grand mal seizures, and shortly after, she died.

Bob Jenkins, her son, told Dr. Black Jack that he would never forgive him.

Five Years Later

Late one evening at approximately 10:00 p.m., Dr. Black Jack and Dr. Joe Shmo were walking home in the bad part of Chicago when they heard a car approaching behind them. At that moment they turned around to see who it was, when the shooting began. The driver of a purple Lamborghini drove up and started shooting a tommy gun in the direction of the two men. Dr. Black Jack was hit immediately and went down; Dr. Joe Shmo was only wounded.

Dr. Shmo was admitted into the hospital for observation, Dr. Black Jack wasn't so lucky. He was pronounced dead at the scene.

Joe decided that once he was released he was going to find out who did this to him and his friend, Jack, because the police didn't seem to be in too big of a hurry to catch the killer.

Immediately after he was released he decided that he would go under cover to find out who did this. He went out and observed what kind of clothing the kids were wearing and then went and purchased some. He got dressed in a Chicago Bulls cap, a large purple and blue striped shirt, a pair of very baggy shorts (size 46—his normal size was 28), a pair of dressed high tennis shoes with a red stripe through them. He wore some wire-rimmed glasses and dyed his hair blond and had his left ear pierced. He wanted to blend in.

He had little information from the police to go on and what he can remember from that night. Someone else had seen the shooting that night and they had seen the purple car, but they noticed something that he didn't. The back left quarter panel of the car was painted green. The house of Jeff Pape was his first stop. Jeff was sitting outside his house when Shmo (cover name) walked up.

Shmo was trying to act cool and talk about the shooting. At first Jeff didn't seem too talkative, but after about an hour, he seemed to open up.

Jeff told Shmo that he had seen it all, the two doctors getting shot, the purple Lamborghini, and the colored paint on the car. I asked him where he was standing during the shooting and he said, "I was in the alley on the right side of the street."

He asked me if I wanted to go get something cold to drink, but I told him that I had to take off, I had an appointment that I would catch up with him later. I needed time to think about what Jeff had told me, it didn't add up. The paint, and where he was standing.

I got back to my apartment and made a list of all the people that would have had a reason to want Dr. Black Jack dead. I ruled out that they were trying to kill me because the driver had a Tommy gun, they were not aiming at me, if they had wanted me dead, I would have been dead.

1. Bob Jenkins—for the murder (accidental death) of his mother
2. Jessie Johnson—a nurse that was fired by Dr. Black Jack
3. Johnny Badluck—pending law suit
4. Jeff Pape—stories don't add up

I began to interview and investigate each one of the suspects. I spoke to Jessie first, she said that she had moved on, she was no longer mad that she was fired. She had found a new job and was very happy.

I already knew Jeff's story, so I would put him on the bottom of my list for now. I tried to contact Bob Jenkins, but he refused to see me. He said that Dr. Black Jack had gotten what he deserved and he felt no remorse for him. I definitely kept him on my list.

I only had to talk to Johnny Badluck and get his story. I found out that he was a member of the blue coats gang and Dr. Black Jack was unable to save Johnny's brother in a gang shooting last year. Johnny blamed Dr. Black Jack saying that it was because he was in a gang and that's why he didn't save him.

I got dressed up in my cover cloths again and went out and found Jeff Pape. We talked for some time and I found out he was a pretty nice kid, just mixed up and had a lot of pain from his father.

For the next couple of days I spent a lot of time under cover trying to get more information about the shooting. To my amazement one day I was walking up the steps to Jeff's apartment when Bob Jenkins came out of the door yelling at Jeff.

I hid in the hall until Jenkins left the building, then went up to talk to Jeff.

I didn't let him know that I knew Jenkins, because I figured that I could get more info by not telling him. By the time I left that night I knew who the murderer was, I just had to prove it.

The next morning I went to the courthouse to get the information that I needed, and next I went to the police with my story.

It took a little convincing the police about my story, but they were willing to go along with the charade to find out who was the murderer.

The police called the suspects in for questioning about the case. Bob Jenkins, Jeff Pape, and Johnny Badluck. In the info I found at the courthouse (old police records) Johnny had quit the gang two months ago, because his best friend was killed in another gang shooting. So I was able to rule out Johnny. It was either Bob or Jeff.

When Jeff entered the room, Bob Jenkins was sitting in a chair on the far side of the room. Jeff asked him what he was doing there. Bob said, "he didn't know why the police had called him in, that they were investigating the murder of Dr. Black Jack." Jeff began to look a little nervous.

I stood up and started asking questions about that night. Jeff wanted to know who I was and why I was asking all the questions. I finally explained to him that I was under cover and that I was really Dr. Joe Shmo and I was there the night of the murder and I know that he was also, but not in the alley where he said he was. I confronted him telling him that he knew the color of the car because he was the driver and that he was the one that killed Dr. Black Jack.

At first Bob Jenkins stood up and said that he couldn't have done it because he doesn't own a car any more. But then Jeff stood up and said, "I did it for you dad, you hated Dr. Jack, for what he did to grandma. I know that you will never marry mom and be my dad all the time but this will help you love me, because I took away the hurt that you were caused your whole life by Dr. Black Jack."

Bob Jenkins took his son in his arms, crying, telling him that he did love him and it didn't matter if his mother and he never got married, he would always be there for him.

Jeff was arrested and had to go in for treatment and therapy. They told him that it would be a long time before he could get out but he would be better when he did.

Dr. Joe Shmo and I went back to my normal life of being a plastic surgeon, but sometimes I kind of miss my sleuthing adventures. And I kept my earring.

Questions for Independent Writing

This assessment gives students the opportunity to reflect on the process of writing a mystery using the Mystery Outline. The questions ask students to provide a rationale for their choice of a crime, setting, characters, and plot development.

1. How did you come up with the crime and its solution?
2. What types of characters did you include in your mystery, and what were their roles?
3. How did you decide to plant the clues?
4. How did you create suspense?
5. Would you like to share your mystery with others?
6. Will you write another mystery?

Mystery Extensions

Included in this section are ideas to extend this mystery unit. Encourage students to delve into the investigative techniques of some famous literary detectives such as Sherlock Holmes, Miss Marple, Dick Tracy, or Nero Wolfe. Or students may wish to enter the real world of investigation and crime by looking into government–employed detective agencies such as Scotland Yard (England), the FBI (USA), or Interpol (International Crime). Another aspect of detective work that may prove fascinating is the training and use of police dogs.

Students also could explore simple number and letter codes. Students could begin their alphabet code with the first letter of their name. For example, using the name "Joe," the alphabet becomes

J K L M N O P Q R S T U V W X Y Z A B C D E F G H I

Joe's name is now spelled "SXN."

To make a different code, students could substitute any letter in the alphabet with the numeral 1 and number successively. For example, the code for the regular alphabet would correspond to the numbers 1 through 26, and Joe's name would be written "10, 15, 5."

As a prewriting activity, you could prepare evidence bags. These are plastic bags, each containing four or five clues including addressed envelopes, tickets, travel brochures, buttons, shells, feathers, coded messages, and anything else that would make a good clue. Small groups of students then try to incorporate and explain all the clues and present an oral mystery with a simple story structure.

Summary

This unit focused on building students' understanding of the important elements in mysteries, including evaluating the type of setting, and identifying the types of characters and their roles. We also discussed plot development, which included building suspense by incorporating cliffhanger chapter endings and presenting clues using foreshadowing and red herrings.

We are now leaving realistic fiction, and journeying into the world of make-believe and the study of traditional literature. The next two units are on traditional literature—folktales, beast tales, cumulative tales, pourquoi stories, and fables.

Chapter Three

Teaching Traditional Folktales

A transformation into a lovely princess, a helpful animal, or a magical object all draw us into a folktale's story line. Folktales are part of our heritage, values, and mores. Good and honest characters go from rags to riches, their problems vanish, and their lives become full of happiness; evil and lazy characters are punished and often banished so we no longer have to worry about them.

Background Information for Teachers

This unit is intended for Grades 3 through 6 and can be customized for each grade level depending on the students' abilities and their background knowledge of the genre. The beginning intermediate students, Grades 3 and 4, can study the basic elements of folktales. Intermediate students, Grades 5 and 6, can learn additional elements that will improve their reading and writing of folktales (see Figure 3.1 on page 56). This section of the unit is designed for the teacher and will explain the literary elements of folktales in detail.

Definition

Traditional literature, according to Tomlison and Lynch–Brown (1996), is "the body of ancient stories and poems that grew out of the human quest to understand the natural and spiritual worlds" (p. 100). These stories also are referred to as fairy tales, but experts who study folktales disagree with this label because some of the stories do not contain fairies. Therefore, we will use the term folktales—stories told by the people.

Figure 3.1   Elements by Level

Beginning Intermediate	Intermediate
Patterned Beginning	Patterned Beginning
Setting	Setting
Characters	Characters
Problem	Problem

Plot—initiating event,
      other events,
      resolution
      and end
	Plot—types of plots,
	      plot development
	      initiating event,
	      other events,
	      resolution and end

Theme	Theme

Storyteller's Style—
      language, magic,
      basic motifs
	Storyteller's Style—
	      language, magic,
	      in–depth motifs

Variant	Variant

Folktales began with the oral tradition and were written down years later. According to Russell (1997), they "originally served a multitude of purposes" (p. 143). He explains that the primary reasons for sharing these tales was to entertain, to teach, to reinforce cultural and social mores, and to explain the creation of the world and its inhabitants. Huck, Helper, Hickman, and Kiefer (1997) state that "originally folklore was the literature of the people; stories were told to young and old alike. Families or tribes or the king's court would gather to hear a famous storyteller" (p. 268). These were the stories of the streets, alleys, fish markets, and countryside. The versions of these tales that have become favorites are credited to the collections of Jakob and Wilhelm Grimm (1812), Charles Perrault (1691), Joseph and Peter Jacobs (1894), and Peter Asbjornsen and Jorgen Moe (1851).

More recently, the Hmong (Laos), who have migrated to the United States, have attempted to preserve the folktales of their culture by writing them down. Charles Johnson (1985), a linguist in Minnesota, spent years with the Hmong people while he translated their stories from Hmong to English in the 1980s. Another author of Hmong folktales, Dia Cha, the coauthor of *Folk Stories of the Hmong* (1991), states that she learned many traditional stories while sitting around the home fire of her native Hmong village in the highlands of Laos and listening to her grandmother, uncles, and aunts. Some years after the Vietnam War ended, the relocation of her family and many other Hmong to the United States affected their traditional ways; she realized the stories were being forgotten. With her book, she has preserved some of these stories in the written form for future generations.

Literary Elements of Folktales

Wonder and beast tales follow the narrative structure, which includes a patterned beginning, setting, characters, a conflict, a quick resolution, and an ending. The storyteller uses the *patterned beginning* to alert the listener that the story will begin and to tell the listener that the story happened a long time ago (Glazer, 1997). The "once upon a time" beginning is familiar to us all and we immediately know what kind of story to expect when we hear this patterned beginning.

Setting in folktales is a backdrop. The term backdrop refers to the scenery on stage for a play at the theater. Lukens (1999) explains that the setting "is generalized and universal; its vividness exists in our minds merely as the place where interesting action occurs" (p. 157). Backdrop settings are used in folktales because although the place is important, the setting does not affect the characters or plot. The setting belongs to the audience listening to the tale; it refers to their forest, village, or country. Therefore, the storyteller does not spend time developing the setting.

Characters in folktales are flat, not well-developed, and stereotypic. The characters "exist as undeveloped types to serve the plot" (Hillman, 1999, p. 68), and their description gives the reader a "clear and immediate picture of the character" (Glazer, 1997, p. 320). These flat characters are either very good or very evil. The good characters are beautiful and kind; the evil characters are ugly and bad. The main character, although good, is usually the underdog. The bad characters may be trolls, giants, and ogres and usually have the advantage through most of the story.

As in other genres, the plot of a folktale develops when a problem is established, and then events follow with the characters' actions in response to these events. As the plot develops, "suspense and action are far more important to these tales than character development" (Russell, 1997, p. 151). Therefore, we are drawn into the story with the actions of the main character. The tale ends abruptly with a quick resolution and a patterned ending—usually, "They lived happily ever after."

FIgure 3.2   Linear Plot Development

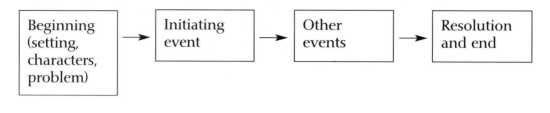

Figure 3.3   Cumulative Plot Development

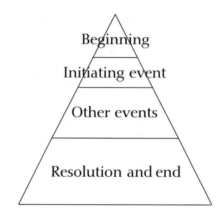

This quick ending is a signal to the listener that the storyteller is finished telling this story.

Plot structure depends on the type of folktale. Animal and wonder tales are organized with a linear plot structure. In the linear plot (see Figure 3.2), a problem is introduced, followed by a series of events as the character attempts to solve the problem. The resolution to the problem is shared, and the story ends.

Cumulative tales are organized using a cumulative plot organization (see Figure 3.3). In this type of plot, the characters, the problem, and characters' actions build onto each other. Jacobs and Tunnel (1996) state that cumulative tales "are 'added upon' as the telling unfolds" (p. 70). In cumulative tales, the story line is not important; the intrigue is in the repetition of phrases. "Typically the story is told up to a certain point, then begun again from near the beginning and told until a new segment is added" (Jacobs & Tunnel, 1996, p. 70). These stories are sometimes called "chain tales," because each part of the story is linked to the next (Cullinan & Galda, 1994, p. 179).

The themes of folktales are reflected in what the culture values. In folktales, good overcomes evil, and this sits well with all of us, because as Huck et al. (1997) share, "values of the culture are expressed in folklore. Humility, kindness, patience, sympathy, hard work, and courage are invariably rewarded" (p. 275). Russell (1997) also sums up the essence of themes in folktales by stating "the virtues of compassion, generosity, and humility [triumphing] over the vices of greed, selfishness, and excessive or overweening pride" are all part of the themes of folktales in Western culture (p. 152). No matter what their country of origin, folktales seem to have universal themes, such as good against evil. Some storytellers delve deeper into this particular theme by identifying the type of good (industrious, kind, patient, clever) and the type of bad (selfish, greedy, lazy). Lukens (1999) states that "the prominence of [theme] in traditional stories seems to verify the human wish to know not only what happened, and how it happened, but also why it happened and what it means" (p. 142).

The storytellers who originally told folktales used language that would hold the listeners' attention and aid the storyteller's memory of the tale. Russell (1997) states that "the language is typically economical, with a minimal amount of description and a heavy reliance on formulaic patterns..." (p. 152). The language contains rhyme, rhythm, repetition, imagery, and sometimes figurative language such as personification, metaphors, and similes.

Original storytellers also included aspects of magic to bring the story out of the realm of the real world and into the make-believe world. In folktales, magic is considered a natural part of everyday life; it is expected. Magic is realized through the use of motifs.

Glazer (1997) writes, "Some characters and certain elements in folktales appear regularly in story after story. The youngest and smallest of siblings is successful after others in the family fail. Wishes are granted. A trickster ends up being the one who is tricked. Magic objects, such as rings, beans, or tablecloths serve as props that are critical to the plot. These elements are called motifs" (pp. 320–321). These are the parts of the story that we all remember. (The motifs that will be shared in this unit are appropriate to use with students in Grades 3 through 6.)

Huck et al. (1997) identified the five most common motifs as magical powers, transformations, magical objects, wishes, and trickery. These authors comment that there are many more motifs in folk literature and suggest that "some motifs have been repeated so frequently that they have been identified as a type of folk story" (p. 276). Examples of stories that have been classified by motif are the talking–animal tales and pourquoi tales. Some motifs also are integral to plot development. For example, the numbers 3, 7, and 12 often appear in folktales. Many tales are organized around the number 3; there are three characters, involved in three events, and three actions.

In this unit, the motifs that will be shared are those identified by Stith Thompson (1955–1958) (see Figure 3.4). To simplify this index of motifs, beginning intermediate students can learn the motifs of animals (talking and magic), magical powers (persons, transformations, magic objects), tests (identification), and trickery (cleverness). Intermediate students can explore the entire index and add some of their own.

A variant is a story that is in the folktale "story family." It shares the same characters, plot, and story line, but includes cultural adaptations. As these stories were passed down by word of mouth from one generation to another, the stories changed as the tale was told. They also were changed to fit the times, the people, the culture, and the customs. These tales are sometimes called "traveling tales" and the different stories are known as variants.

Narrative theorists have studied variants and the progression of their telling over many generations and cultures and have found that the most salient parts survive. Huck, et al (1997) state that "each variant has basically the same story or plot as another, but it might have different characters and a different setting or it might use different motifs" (p. 278). This aspect of variants was recognized by Charles Johnson (1985) when he started to preserve Hmong stories. He states, "Oral literature, by its very nature, exists in variant forms. We have seen, for example, nine versions of the Hmong myth of the Great Flood, all of them different, varying widely in details as to what caused the flood, who the survivors were, how they were saved. All the versions are variants and have evolved through many retellings across centuries of time" (p. xvi).

Variety Within the Genre

Beast or animal tales, wonder tales, legends, tall tales, myths, realistic tales, noodlehead tales, cumulative tales, pourquoi tales, and fables—all of these categories fall under the genre of folktales. In this unit, we will concentrate on the elements of beast tales, wonder tales, and cumulative tales. Pourquoi tales and fables are discussed in Chapter Four.

Figure 3.4   Common Motifs in Folktales

Animals
Magic
Talking
Friendly
     helpful
     grateful
     provide services

Magic
Magical powers
Transformations
     man to man
     man to animal
     man to object
     animal to person
Magical objects
     ownership
     kinds
     functions
     characteristics
     who possesses

Trickery
Wise and unwise
Cleverness
Deceptions
     contests won
     escape
     capture
     falls into trap

Test
     Identification
     Truth
     Cleverness
     Endurance
     Survival

Supernatural
Marvels
     fairies
     elves
     remarkable entities
Extraordinary powers
     ogre
     giants
Amazing places and things

Beast tales or animal tales are tales in which animals talk and act like humans, not as animals. Common motifs found in these tales include talking animals and trickery. Some examples in this category are "The Three Little Pigs," "The Little Red Hen," "Puss in Boots," and "The Three Billy Goats Gruff."

Cumulative tales are tales in which events build upon one another. Usually the tale starts with one initiating event and the other events chain onto this first event. While building this chain, each event is repeated until the end. Common motifs found in these tales are talking animals and magic objects. Some examples in this category are *The Mitten* (1989) retold by Jan Brett, *The Gingerbread Boy* (1984) retold by Paul Galdone and *Bringing the Rain to Kapiti Plain* (1981) and "Goso the Teacher" (1994) retold by Verna Aardema.

Wonder tales revolve around magical creatures and supernatural powers. The characters could include fairy godmothers, handsome princes, magical objects or beings, and the most common motifs are trickery and transformations of people, animals, or objects. There is universal appeal for these stories because all ends well, evil is punished, and the main characters live "happily ever after." Some examples of wonder tales include "Cinderella," "Sleeping Beauty," "Beauty and the Beast," "Snow White," and "Jack and the Beanstalk."

Teaching the Traditional Folktale

Pre–Read-Aloud Activities

To begin the unit on folktales, hold a brainstorming session to find out what students already know about this genre. Record the results of the brainstorming session on a chart in the classroom and ask students to revise and update the chart as they become familiar with folktales. A Mixed–Up Folktales Quiz (see Figure 3.5) is appropriate for students in Grades 3 and 4 because the quiz focuses on the story line. A Folktales by Country Quiz (see Figure 3.6) is appropriate for students in Grades 5 and 6 because the quiz focuses on the cultural aspects of the folktales. If students do not know the answers, invite them to read the folktales highlighted in their quiz.

To help students understand the elements of folktales, several books may be selected for a whole–class read–aloud. While reading these folktales, demonstrate and apply the elements through teaching strategies. The following charts can be designed prior to the read–aloud: Folktale Plot Map (page 65), Storyteller's Style Chart (page 67), Motif Chart (page 68), and Comparing Variants (page 70).

The folktale that will be used in this unit is *Wishbones: A Folktale from China* (1993), retold by Barbara Ker Wilson, which follows a linear plot

Figure 3.5 Mixed-Up Folktales Quiz

These folktales are mixed up. Can you fix the underlined part so that it is correct?

1. Cinderella wanted to go to <u>a birthday party</u>.
2. The Twelve Dancing Princesses wore <u>roller skates</u>.
3. Sleeping Beauty was awakened <u>by the alarm clock</u>.
4. The Three Billy Goats Gruff wanted to cross <u>the Atlantic Ocean</u>.
5. Hansel and Gretel met a <u>troll by the bridge</u>.
6. Jack climbed up <u>an apple tree</u>.
7. The Three Little Pigs built <u>an apartment house</u>.
8. Little Red–Riding Hood went to visit <u>the wicked witch</u>.
9. Rapunzel had long <u>fingernails</u>.
10. Aladdin made wishes after he rubbed <u>his head</u> three times.

Answers: 1. the ball; 2. slippers; 3. by a prince's kiss; 4. the bridge; 5. witch by her house of goodies; 6. a beanstalk; 7. a house of straw, one of sticks, and one of bricks; 8. her grandmother; 9. hair; 10. a magic lamp.

Figure 3.6 Folktales by Country Quiz

Folktales come from all over the world. Many of our old favorites were first told in another country. Many countries heard a tale and then changed it so it fit their own culture and traditions. Can you match the folktales to their correct country of origin?

1. Jack and the Beanstalk	A. China
2. Strega Nona	B. England
3. Baboushka	C. Arabia
4. Cinderella	D. Africa
5. Aladdin and the Wonderful Lamp	E. Germany
6. Rough–Face Girl	F. Russia
7. Mufaro's Beautiful Daughters	G. Native American
8. Lon Po Po: A Red–Riding Hood Story	H. France
9. Snow White & the Seven Dwarfs	I. Italy

Answers: 1. B; 2. I; 3. F; 4. H; 5. C; 6. G; 7. D; 8. A; 9. E structure, but the activities we will discuss are suitable for most folktales. If you choose to teach cumulative tales, use the elements discussed in the Background Information for Teachers section of this chapter. (See page 160 of the bibliography for more folktales to discuss with your class.)

Read-Aloud Activities

Help students develop a deeper understanding of the elements of folktales by modeling the story structure, theme, and the storyteller's style through the read–aloud and by using teaching strategies illustrated in this section.

Following the Plot

The questions and activities suggested below will help students identify the differences between a linear plot and a cumulative plot.

1. What type of plot structure is used in this tale?
2. What is the problem of the main character?
3. What is the initiating event that starts the main character's action?
4. What are the other events in this story?
5. What is the resolution?
6. How does the tale end?

"Wishbones," our folktale read–aloud, is organized with a linear plot structure. The Folktale Plot Map (see Figure 3.7), will help students visualize plot structure.

Determining one problem may confuse students, because the main character in *Wishbones* seems to have a multitude of problems: Yeh-Hsien is discriminated against by her stepmother, her father seems helpless in dealing with her stepmother, and her stepmother kills her pet fish. The last straw and the main problem is that her stepmother kills her fish—Yeh-Hsien's favorite thing.

In this story, the initiating event is the visit from the old man, who tells Yeh-Hsien to find the bones of the fish because they are magic. Use a Folktale Plot Map to illustrate the initiating event and the events that follow (see Figure 3.7). This map is for *Wishbones*.

Evaluating the Setting

Folktales usually begin with a patterned beginning such as "Once upon a time," followed by a quick introduction that creates a backdrop setting, identifies the flat characters, and presents a one-dimensional problem. The following questions will help students identify the storytelling device of patterned beginnings and evaluate backdrop settings.

1. When does the story take place? How do you know this?
2. Where does the story take place?
3. Is the story's setting important to the story's action? Why or why not?

Setting may be found in the first sentence of a folktale. Our read-aloud takes place in China, thousands of years ago. This is a backdrop setting that is not important to the story because the listeners already know where the story takes place; it is a story about the history of their life, culture, or country.

Figure 3.7   Folktale Plot Map

Initiating Event: Old man visits and tells Yeh–Hsien of magic bones
Actions: Wishes on bones for jewels and fine robes

Event: Festival—family leaves her home
Actions: Dresses up and goes to festival

Event: Afraid she was recognized
Actions: Runs away and silken slipper falls off

Event: King buys slipper and searches for owner
Actions: She tries on slipper

Resolution: Marries King
King misuses fish bones, buries fish bone
Patterned Ending: "They have never been found to this day."

Identifying the Types of Characters

The main character in a folktale is usually good, and the supporting characters are usually bad. The questions below will help students identify the types of characters found in folktales.

1. Who is the main character in this tale?
2. Who are the other characters?
3. What do we know about the main character?
4. Who are the good and bad characters in this story?

The main character in *Wishbones* is Yeh–Hsien and the other characters are her father, stepmother, stepsisters, and her pet fish. The information that the storyteller shares will lead the students to an understanding of a flat character. In the first few pages, we find out about the main character, Yeh–Hsien:

> Her mother died.
> Her father loves her.
> Her stepmother is unkind and dislikes her because she is beautiful.
> She is forced to do chores in dangerous places.
> She catches a fish.
> She feeds the fish and the fish becomes big.
> She moves the fish to a pond.
> She wears shabby clothes.

From this information, we conclude that Yeh–Hsien is a good person, loved by her father and disliked by her stepmother. Not much else is shared about the main character, which leads us to label Yeh–Hsien as a flat, undeveloped character. We learn much less about the other characters, however. To determine the good and bad characters, students could make a list of each characters' traits.

Realizing the Theme

Now students will explore why this tale was told. The following questions will guide students to realizing the theme. The theme for *Wishbones* is good overcoming evil or selflessness overcoming greediness.

1. What happened in this folktale?
2. How did it happen?
3. Why did it happen?
4. What does this mean to you? (This is the theme!)

Figure 3.8   Storyteller's Style Chart

Language:

Imagery:

Figurative Language:

    Personification:

    Similes:

    Metaphors:

Storyteller's Style

In this section, a question and an activity help the students to listen for imagery, repetition, rhyme, and figurative language. After listening to the story, students can record the most memorable language from the story on the Storyteller's Style Chart (see Figure 3.8).

Ask students, did the storyteller use language that held your attention? To answer this question, have students collect phrases or sentences that were attractive to them as they listened.

Recognizing Motifs

Storytellers add magic and fantasy to folktales. By recognizing the motifs in folklore, students will gain a better understanding of how and why authors use motifs. (See Common Motifs in Folktales in Figure 3.4 on page 61). To understand the aspects of magic and motifs, the class could revisit the list that was generated during the brainstorming session at the beginning of the unit. The ideas that students listed as already known about folktales could be put into categories and then organized on a semantic map. For example, one third–grade classroom came up with this list of what they already knew about folktales: "Once upon a time," animals, people, castles, "Lived happily ever after,"

Figure 3.9 Motif Chart

Story:	Patterned Beginning	Animals	Magical Powers	Magic Objects	Trickery	Trans- formations	Tests
Wish- bones	+	+	+	+	+		+
Yeh- Shen	+	+	+	+	+	+	+

dragons, magical things, "Long ago," witches, good and bad, beasts, princesses, princes, queens, kings, goblins, black cats, water, fish, monsters, far away places. These items could be grouped on a chart using these categories: settings, good characters, bad characters, motifs, patterned beginnings and endings. The Motif Chart (Figure 3.9) will help students answer the question and chart story motifs. Ask students, what motifs were included in this story?

For the folktales you choose to read aloud, students can develop a Motif Chart like the one in Figure 3.9. The motifs for *Wishbones* can be placed on the chart now, and when a variant is shared, the class can revisit the Motif Chart and add the motifs for that story.

Understanding Variants

In this section, by answering the questions and completing the activities, students will learn how variants originate. To illustrate the concept of a variant—a story that changes as different storytellers tell it—share another version of *Wishbones*, a Chinese tale called *Yeh-Shen: A Cinderella Story from China* (1982) by Ai-Ling Louie. (Any two variants of a folktale can be used for this activity.) As you read the second tale to the class, ask students to make a comparison chart of all the elements of each story. (See Figure 3.10 on page 70 for an example of this chart.) Ask the following questions about the variants:

1. What are the stories' countries of origin?
2. Did the storytellers use the same patterned beginning and ending?

3. Are the characters the same in both stories?

4. Is the setting the same?

5. What is the main character's conflict in the two stories?

6. What is the initiating event that starts the action of the main character in these two tales?

7. Are the subsequent events the same in both tales?

8. What is the resolution and the ending?

9. Did both storytellers use the same imagery and figurative language?

10. Did both storytellers use the same motifs?

11. Which story did you enjoy more, and why did you enjoy this story more than the other?

Small-Group Guided Reading

Now give students the opportunity to read and explore other folk-tales in the categories that were mentioned in this unit such as beast tales and cumulative tales. The questions and instructional activities shared during the read–aloud can be used during the small–group guided reading of folktales.

Allow students to select a folktale to read in small groups. Students have worked through the questions and activities with you as a model, so now they should feel comfortable using the same questions and activities in small groups. Help students decide what strategies to repeat, and students should add their own questions for discussion.

While reading in their groups, students can fill in charts like Mapping a Folktale (page 74), Linear or Cumulative Tale Planner (page 65 or 75), Storyteller's Style Chart, Motif Chart, and Comparing Variants.

During small–group time, students may choose to fill in all the charts or only those that helped them understand folktales during the read–aloud.

Questions for Small-Group Guided Reading

Ask students these questions in their small guided–reading groups:

1. How did your group decide which questions and activities to use? Were your questions and activities effective in helping you understand folktales?

Figure 3.10   Comparing Variants

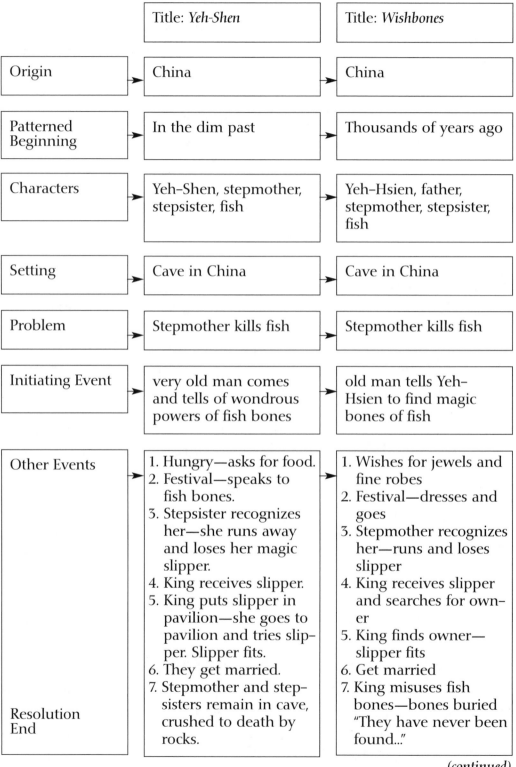

	Title: *Yeh-Shen*	Title: *Wishbones*
Origin	China	China
Patterned Beginning	In the dim past	Thousands of years ago
Characters	Yeh–Shen, stepmother, stepsister, fish	Yeh–Hsien, father, stepmother, stepsister, fish
Setting	Cave in China	Cave in China
Problem	Stepmother kills fish	Stepmother kills fish
Initiating Event	very old man comes and tells of wondrous powers of fish bones	old man tells Yeh–Hsien to find magic bones of fish
Other Events Resolution End	1. Hungry—asks for food. 2. Festival—speaks to fish bones. 3. Stepsister recognizes her—she runs away and loses her magic slipper. 4. King receives slipper. 5. King puts slipper in pavilion—she goes to pavilion and tries slipper. Slipper fits. 6. They get married. 7. Stepmother and stepsisters remain in cave, crushed to death by rocks.	1. Wishes for jewels and fine robes 2. Festival—dresses and goes 3. Stepmother recognizes her—runs and loses slipper 4. King receives slipper and searches for owner 5. King finds owner—slipper fits 6. Get married 7. King misuses fish bones—bones buried "They have never been found..."

(continued)

Figure 3.10   Comparing Variants (continued)

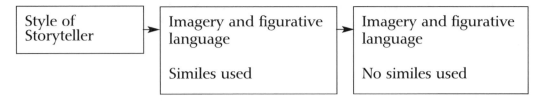

2. What information did you find in the patterned beginning?

3. Who were the good and the bad characters in the story?

4. What was the problem in the story?

5. What was the cultural heritage of the story? How do you know this?

6. What motifs were used in the story?

Independent Writing of Folktales

When students write their own folktales, they will see the whole structure of this genre.

As students plan the writing of their own folktale, several techniques might be useful. Beginning intermediate students can create a Wordless Picture Book. Give students the book's format (see Figure 3.11) and instruct them to plan their folktale by illustrating its elements. The Wordless Picture Book in Figure 3.11 was developed by Justine, a third grader, before she mapped out her story.

Another technique that students may find useful in planning their folktale is the Plot Cube (see Figure 3.12). Neeld (1986), designed this cubing activity to use with expository text, but we have revised this activity to fit narrative text.

Intermediate students will benefit from Mapping a Folktale (see Figure 3.13 on page 74), an outline that allows students to create their stories before they begin to write. Alert students to the idea of writing their story from a storyteller's perspective, that their tale should have a theme to communicate (such as overcoming adversity, achieving autonomy, or coping with family problems), and that their tale happened in a particular country a long time ago.

When this folktale unit was taught in a third–grade classroom, Justine planned her folktale by using the Wordless Picture Book, drafted the ideas using the Plot Cube, and then wrote her folktale.

Figure 3.11   Justine's Wordless Picture Book

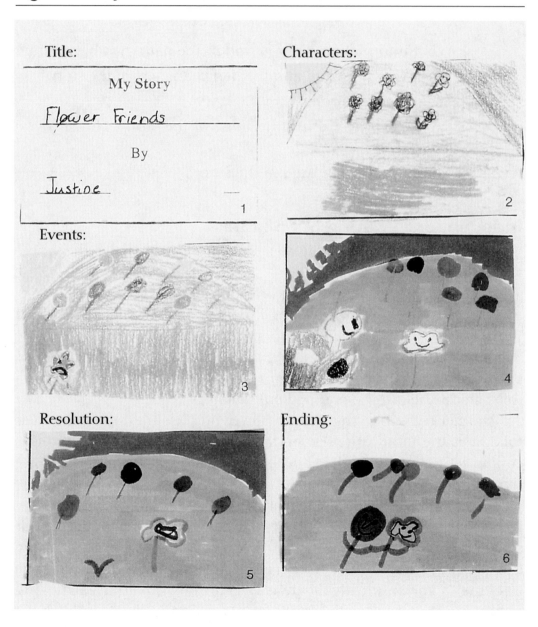

Figure 3.12   Plot Cube

	Characters	
Solution	Setting	End
	Problem	
	Actions	

Flower Friends
by Justine

Once in a far away meadow there lived a girl flower. She had not one friend and longed for one, for all the other flowers talked on the green hill.

Oh, how she wished to have a friend to live by.

One day a boy dug a hole next to her. Next he dropped a seed in it. Then he buried it. He watered it and left. In a week she had a friend. And they told each other about themselves. And they lived happily ever after.

Figure 3.13 Mapping a Folktale

1. Decide what you want to tell others.
2. Decide where your story will take place.
3. Decide on at least four characters:
   a. A good main character.
   b. An evil, bad character.
   c. One special character.
   d. One other character.
4. Decide on the problem of the main character.
5. Decide on an initiating event—the event that will start the character into action.
6. Plan the other events, including the actions of the main character.
7. Decide what motifs you will include in your story.
8. Design the outline for your folktale.
   a. Beginning: patterned beginning, setting, characters, and statement of one problem.
   b. Middle: initiating event and subsequent events; decide how you will include the motifs.
   c. Ending: how will the problem of the main character be resolved? Plan a patterned ending.

This unit was also taught in a fourth-grade classroom. The folktale written by Coral and Teresa follows:

The Witches and the Three Cats
by Coral and Teresa

Once upon a time there were three cats that lived in the same alley. There were two witches: Hilda, the bad witch, and Lucy, the good witch who wanted to be a bad witch. So they both looked in their magic books to find the potion to make the change.

Lucy saw that she needed two cats' heads to make the potion. Yuck! She got her broom and set out looking for two cats. Hilda saw that she needed one whole cat, and she laughed and got out her dirty broom and set out looking.

Lucy got off her broom because she heard a meow in the alley. She looked around and found two cats. She put them in a bag and took them to her home. Hilda came to the same alley and found a cat. She put the cat in her extra shirt and took the cat to her home. Lucy almost cut off their heads but one of the cats said, "Wait!" She quickly stopped. The other cat quickly went to the magic book. The cat said, "The potion needs cats that don't talk." But it really said just the opposite. She believed them, so she let them go. Hilda picked up the cat, but the cat said, "I would be bad for the potion. Look in my bag, there is a better cat there." Hilda looked in. She saw a cat but she didn't know it was not a real cat. So she let it go. The other cats found each other and they lived happily ever after, but not the witches.

A unit on cumulative tales was taught in a fourth–grade classroom. Andrea first planned her story using the Cumulative Tale Planner (see Figure 3.14) and then wrote her story.

Figure 3.14   Andrea's Cumulative Tale Planner

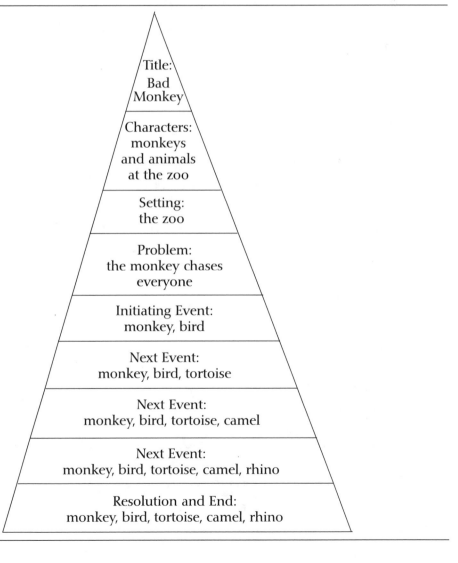

Bad Monkey
by Andrea

Once there was a monkey who was Harris Sassy. He was an enthusiastic monkey who chased a feathery bird because he was misbehaving. The enthusiastic monkey chased a feathery bird who bit the lazy tortoise who yelped oowwll because he was sensitive. The enthusiastic monkey who chased a feathery bird as she bit the lazy tortoise, who crashed into the camel because he was too lazy to prevent it from happening. The enthusiastic monkey chased the feathery bird who bit the lazy tortoise who crashed into the grouchy camel and bumped into the polite rhino because he was grouchy. The enthusiastic monkey chased the feathery bird who bit the lazy tortoise who crashed into the grouchy camel when he bumped into the polite rhino as he charged at the ragged hippo because he couldn't help himself. The enthusiastic monkey chased the feathery bird who bit the lazy tortoise as she crashed into the grouchy camel and bumped into the polite rhino who charged at the ragged hippo, so the hippo decided to bite the monkey because he was trying to take a nap. Now the monkey only chases monkeys.

Questions for Writing Folktales

The following questions give students the opportunity to reflect on the process of writing a folktale. The questions ask students to provide rationale for their choices of patterned beginnings, settings, characters, and motifs.

1. Did you include a patterned beginning and ending in your folktale?
2. Did you include a setting for your story?
3. Did you include both good and bad characters in your folktale?
4. Would you like to share your folktale with others?
5. Will you write another folktale?

Traditional Folktale Extensions

The ideas included in this section are intended to extend the Traditional Folktale Unit. Invite students to collect stories from their families—including parents, grandparents, aunts, or uncles—to share orally with the class.

Students also might enjoy rewriting a folktale into a Readers Theatre script. The following sequence could be used to illustrate that folktales are passed down by word of mouth and then are written down:

1. Share the folktale orally with others.
2. Make a copy of it.
3. Mark the dialogue using a different color for each speaker.
4. Read the folktale and decide which text parts need to be read by a narrator. Underline these parts in a different color.
5. Decide who will say the parts.
6. Perform the folktale.

Students could design a story cloth similar to those made by the Hmong. A Story Cloth is an illustrative cloth in which the illustrations represent the events of the folktale. Students could use fabric markers on muslin for a small group project.

Summary

Studying traditional literature begins a journey into the oral tradition of storytelling. Through the study of folktales, students learn how storytellers begin and end stories, how they create settings, and why they use flat characters and one-dimensional problems. Students are also exposed to the storyteller's quick and repetitive use of language that takes us into the make-believe world with motifs. The journey continues across cultures as students learn about variants, or the traveling tales, from many cultures. Our next unit focuses on two other subgenres of traditional literature, pourquoi stories and fables.

Chapter Four

Teaching Pourquoi Stories and Fables

Two important subgenres of traditional literature are pourquoi stories and fables, which have been passed through oral tradition and whose authors are usually unknown.

Background Information for Teachers

As in previous chapters, this unit is intended for Grades 3 through 6, and Figure 4.1 explains how you can customize the unit to fit your students' needs and abilities. Beginning intermediate students may find it easier to write a pourquoi story, while intermediate students may enjoy the more complex form of the fable.

Figure 4.1   Elements by Level

Beginning Intermediate	Intermediate
Pourquoi Story	Fable
Beginnings—patterned	Beginnings—patterned
Setting—backdrop	Setting—backdrop
Characters—flat, stereotypic	Characters—flat, stereotypic
Problem—one dimensional	Problem—one dimensional
Plot—actions to answer stated question	Plot—actions to prove moral
End—short, patterned, states why things are the way they are today	End—states the moral
	Author's Style—dialogue, personification

Definition of a Pourquoi Story

The word *pourquoi* means "why" in French. Pourquoi stories are short narratives that have been passed orally in all cultures to provide an explanation for creation, nature's elements, people's actions, and animal characteristics. Pourquoi stories are sometimes mistakenly classified as myths, but, as Tomlison and Lynch–Brown (1996) explain, "deities play no role in pourquoi tales as they do in myths. Moreover, the setting is earthly, while the setting in myths is the realm of the gods" (p. 109).

Literary Elements of Pourquoi Stories

The story structure of a pourquoi tale follows the narrative structure and includes descriptions of time, characters, problem, actions of characters, resolution, and ending.

Patterned beginnings emphasize the time of the story rather than the setting of the tale and are used to alert listeners that the story has begun.

Setting, if given, usually emphasizes a culture or a country. It is a backdrop setting because the storyteller assumes that everyone knows the setting. The setting can be derived from illustrations if the story is in book form.

Characters are either animals, people, or nature. The characters are flat because everyone knows what an elephant, a person from their village, or a palm tree is like, so these characters do not need a lot of explanation. Animals and people are often presented stereotypically. There is usually one main character and other supporting characters; the main character will change by the end of the story.

The **conflict** is one–dimensional and centers on why or how something changed from the way it used to be to how it is today.

Plot development is linear and revolves around the character's actions to solve the question of how or why. The main character usually receives help from other supporting characters. The resolution should lead us to the answer to the question, and the end is short and sometimes patterned.

Variety Within the Genre

Pourquoi stories can be classified by the character, inanimate or animate, being explained:

People or a person as the main character stories include an explanation of the characteristics of a group of people. Some examples are "Why Farmers Have to Carry Their Crops" (1985) edited by Charles Johnson, "How People Hunted the Moose" (1992) by Joseph Bruchac, and "Why the Hmong Live on Mountains" (1991) retold by Norma Livo and Dia Cha.

Nature as the main character stories provide an explanation of creation or the attributes of a specific force of nature. Some examples are *Why the Tides Ebb and Flow* (1979) by Joan Bowden, and "How Oceans Came to Be" (1976) by Diane Orosco.

Animal as the main character stories explain animal characteristics. Some examples are *Why Mosquitoes Buzz in People's Ears* (1975) by Verna Aardema and "Why the Snake Has No Legs" (1976) by Peggy Appiah.

Often pourquoi stories are collected from different cultures and published in anthologies about one culture. Students can read these stories to develop an understanding of how and where people live and what they value.

Teaching the Pourquoi Story

To begin the unit on pourquoi stories, hold a brainstorming session with the class to determine what students already know about this genre and record the results on a chart in the classroom. As students become more familiar with this genre, the chart can be revised and updated. Then discuss questions students might have about their environment, beginning each with the word *why* or *how*. After they have had a chance to list some questions they have wondered about, tell students that early cultures asked questions also. Storytellers attempted to answer these questions through a story because they did not possess scientific information.

After the brainstorming session is completed, you may want to give a preview test that asks students to formulate a question and to answer it with a story. Have students read the beginning of a story, then state the "how" or "why" question that will be answered. Then ask students to give a synopsis of a story that will answer the question. An example is provided in Figure 4.2.

To develop an understanding of the elements of pourquoi stories, choose a story to read aloud to the whole class. (Because pourquoi sto-

Figure 4.2   Questions and Causes Quiz

Beginning	How or Why	Cause
When the earth was young, all animals could talk to one another.	Why can't they talk any more?	Because they kept getting into fights and teasing other species so now they can't talk to one another just to their own species.
A long time ago, fish lived on land.		
In the beginning, the sun and moon lived on earth.		
Many, many years ago, there were no stars in the sky.		
In the early days of the world all bears were brown, even the polar bear.		
In the beginning of time, trees never lost their leaves.		

ries are short, you may want to share one or two for background knowledge of this subgenre before working through the teaching techniques.) If the pourquoi story you share is available in a picture book, discuss how the illustrations add to the story. While reading this pourquoi story, help students learn the elements by demonstrating and applying them through the teaching strategies.

Read-Aloud Activities

Help students understand the structure of pourquoi stories by introducing the elements and the structure of these tales using the Pourquoi Map (see Figure 4.3 on page 85).

The pourquoi story that will be modeled in this unit is a Nigerian folktale, *Why the Sky is Far Away: A Nigerian Folktale* (1992), as told by Mary-Joan Gerson. It is an appropriate read aloud for either beginning intermediate or intermediate students. However, all activities and questions used in this unit are suitable for most pourquoi stories, so you may choose any tale that you know well and that is appropriate for your grade level. (See the bibliography of pourquoi stories on page 164 for additional book possibilities.)

Understanding Patterned Beginnings

The patterned beginning is used by the storyteller in pourquoi stories to alert the listener that the story will begin. You'll recall that in traditional folktales a patterned beginning tells the listener that the story happened a long time ago, or "Once upon a time." In pourquoi stories, the patterned beginning is equally as short and emphasizes the time of the story rather than the setting. It usually explains how the world was different many years ago. Examples of patterned beginnings in pourquoi stories might be "One cold, dark winter," or "One day when the earth was new," or in this beginning from *How the Stars Fell into the Sky* (1992) by Jerrie Oughton, "When the pulse of the first day carried it to the rim of night, First Woman said to First Man 'The people need to know the laws…'" (p. 6).

Once they understand patterned beginnings, students will be able to identify when the story took place. In our read–aloud, the story begins:

"In the beginning, the sky was very close to the earth."

Evaluating Setting

By using the author's notes, subtitles, pictures, and the questions below, students will be able to evaluate the setting:

1. How do you know where this story took place?
2. Do the illustrations give a clue to the culture or country of origin?

In *Why the Sky is Far Away*, the text only tells us that this is a society that weaves, carves, retells tales, and prepares festivals because they do not need to sow and harvest crops and they do not need to cook. To answer these questions, you may need to look at the cover and the author's note at the back of the book. In our read–aloud example, the illustrations by Carla Golembe show colorfully dressed, black–skinned people who live in huts in a warm climate. The author's note tells us that the folktale was first told in the language of the Bini tribe of Nigeria at least 500 years ago.

Identifying Types of Characters

Answering the questions in this section will help students to identify the main character and the supporting characters.

1. Who or what is the main character?
2. What do we know about this character?
3. Who are the supporting characters and why do they appear in the pourquoi tale?

There are two main characters in our read–aloud. The sky is the character who will change during the tale. The other character is presented stereotypically. She is a woman who is never satisfied, but wants more jewelry, children, and food.

The supporting characters in *Why the Sky is Far Away* are the people of the village and the king, all of whom provide the tale's problem and move the action of the story along.

Clarifying the Conflict

A pourquoi story's conflict may be stated as a question in the title or the text. The questions in this section help students clarify the problem.

1. How was the earth different long ago?
2. What was the problem?

Often the first few sentences of the tale give a description of the earth as it was. In our read–aloud, the earth was very different from today's world; the sky was so close to the earth that people used to reach up and eat pieces of it.

> In that time, men and women did not have to sow crops and harvest them. They did not have to prepare soup and cook rice. The children did not have to carry water from the stream or gather sticks for the fire. Anybody who was hungry just reached up, took a piece of sky, and ate it. It was delicious, too.

The problem explains why this scenario had to change.

> But the sky was growing angry because people were wasteful. Most often they took more than they could possibly eat and threw the leftovers onto garbage heaps. (pages not numbered)

Following Plot Development

Use the following questions and activity to help students follow the plot to discover the story's reason for why the world is the way it is today.

1. What actions of the characters culminate in the change between the world as it was and the world that we know?
2. What is the resolution?
3. How does the tale end?
4. What do we learn at the end of the story?

In *Why the Sky is Far Away*, Sky warns the king that if people continue to waste the gifts provided, the gifts will no longer be there for the people. The selfish woman, after a festival, reaches up and breaks off a large piece of sky. She cannot finish eating it and buries it in the garbage.

Our read-aloud's resolution takes place when the ground shakes with thunder, lightning flashes and Sky moves away from the people. To find out how the tale ends, we only have to look at the world today; people are now forced to grow their own food.

A pourquoi story's ending tells the listener how things are now. The ending in pourquoi stories is not the same as the patterned ending of folktales, though they both serve the same purpose: to tell listeners that the story is over. A good example of a patterned ending can be found in the book *How the Stars Fell into the Sky* (Oughton, 1992), which ends, "As the pulse of the second day brought it into being, the people rose and went about their lives, never knowing in what foolish haste Coyote had tumbled the stars...never knowing the reason for the confusion that would always dwell among them" (pp. 30–31). There is a short patterned ending to our read-aloud:

"And far above them rested the sky, distant and blue, just as it does today." (pages not numbered)

To organize the parts of a pourquoi tale, have students complete a Pourquoi Map (see Figure 4.3).

Small-Group Guided Reading

Give students the opportunity to read and explore other pourquoi tales. Use the questions and the instructional activities shared during the read-aloud with the small-group guided reading.

Figure 4.3   Pourquoi Map

My question is my title.

```
┌─────────────────────────────────────────────────┐
│                                                   │
│                                                   │
│                                                   │
└─────────────────────────────────────────────────┘
```

The patterned beginning tells when and how things used to be.

```
┌─────────────────────────────────────────────────┐
│                                                   │
│                                                   │
│                                                   │
└─────────────────────────────────────────────────┘
```

The characters are flat and stereotypic.

```
┌─────────────────────────────────────────────────┐
│                                                   │
│                                                   │
│                                                   │
└─────────────────────────────────────────────────┘
```

The problem is how the world used to be and why it changed.

```
┌─────────────────────────────────────────────────┐
│                                                   │
│                                                   │
│                                                   │
└─────────────────────────────────────────────────┘
```

The actions move the story along.

```
┌─────────────────────────────────────────────────┐
│                                                   │
│                                                   │
│                                                   │
└─────────────────────────────────────────────────┘
```

The resolution explains why the world is the way it is now.

```
┌─────────────────────────────────────────────────┐
│                                                   │
│                                                   │
│                                                   │
└─────────────────────────────────────────────────┘
```

Encourage students to add to the list of questions used during the read–aloud. During this group time, students choose a pourqoui tale to read and then fill in the Pourquoi Map.

Questions for Small-Group Guided Reading of Pourquoi Stories

 1. How did your group decide on the questions and activities that you would use? Were your choices effective in helping you understand pourquoi stories?

2. Where and when did your pourquoi story take place? How do you know?

3. According to the story, how was the world different a long time ago?

4. According to the story, why did the world change to how it is today?

Independent Writing of Pourquoi Stories

Students will see the whole structure of this genre by writing pourquoi stories themselves, following the prewriting, drafting, revising, editing, and publishing processes of writing. To help students organize their writing, ask them to brainstorm three questions they have. Have students complete a Pourquoi Map for Writing to plan their tale (see Figure 4.4), then develop their map.

Robbie, a fourth-grade student, brainstormed three or four questions that he wondered about, and then used this map to plan his story.

Robbie's Map

My question is my title.
> Why the leopard has spots

A patterned beginning tells when and how things used to be.
> When the first animals were living, all the animals had dull-colored hide.

Who are the characters?
> Leopard, elephant, tiger

What is the problem?
> No one would paint leopard's hide because they were bad artists.

What actions are tried to solve the problem?
> Fell in paints

How is the main character changed?
> Has spots

Patterned ending and how things are now.
> From then on the leopard has spots and chases the other animals for not painting him.

Figure 4.4   Pourquoi Maps for Writing

My question is my title.

```
┌─────────────────────────────────────────────────────────┐
│                                                           │
│                                                           │
│                                                           │
└─────────────────────────────────────────────────────────┘
```

A patterned beginning tells when and how things used to be.

```
┌─────────────────────────────────────────────────────────┐
│                                                           │
│                                                           │
│                                                           │
└─────────────────────────────────────────────────────────┘
```

What is the problem?

```
┌─────────────────────────────────────────────────────────┐
│                                                           │
│                                                           │
│                                                           │
└─────────────────────────────────────────────────────────┘
```

What actions are tried to solve the problem?

```
┌─────────────────────────────────────────────────────────┐
│                                                           │
│                                                           │
│                                                           │
└─────────────────────────────────────────────────────────┘
```

How is the main character changed?

```
┌─────────────────────────────────────────────────────────┐
│                                                           │
│                                                           │
│                                                           │
└─────────────────────────────────────────────────────────┘
```

A patterned ending tells how things are now.

```
┌─────────────────────────────────────────────────────────┐
│                                                           │
│                                                           │
│                                                           │
└─────────────────────────────────────────────────────────┘
```

Robbie drafted his pourquoi story using the planning map and published it. Here is his story:

Why the Leopard Has Spots
by Robbie

When the first animals were living, all the animals had dull colored hides. This was a problem because they were jealous of all the bright colored stuff.

But one day, they found a trunk of paints. Leopard, being the best artist, was forced to paint the other animals' hides. Elephant was painted a bright gray, which dulled over the years. Lion was painted a bright gold. Moose was painted dark brown. Tiger was painted orange with black stripes. But no one would paint leopard.

Leopard was walking around the paints thinking about what to do, when he tripped over a rock and fell into the paints. From then on, he had spots, which also explains why the leopard chases, kills, and eats the other animals.

Questions for Writing Pourquoi Stories

This assessment gives students an opportunity to reflect on the process of writing a pourquoi story following the Pourquoi Map. The questions ask students to provide a rationale for their choices of a patterned beginning, basic questions, and the world as it was long ago and is today.

1. Did you start with a patterned beginning that stated either a time or a place?
2. How did you decide on your question?
3. How did you describe the world as it used to be?
4. Does your resolution also contain a description of the world as it is today?

Definition of a Fable

A fable is a short story that teaches a lesson. As Sutherland (1997) writes, a fable is a "brief narrative which takes abstract ideas of behavior—good or bad, wise or foolish—and attempts to make them concrete and striking enough to be understood and remembered" (p. 205). Fables are distinguished from other traditional literature because they contain a moral that is stated explicitly at the end. Many fables were told by storytellers, so we do not know their authors, but some of the earliest fables were told between 620 and 560 B.C. and are credited to Aesop. La Fontaine brought fables to France.

Literary Elements of Fables

The story structure of fables follows the narrative structure, which includes a short beginning, setting, characters, problem, action of characters to solve the problem, and a resolution. A fable is unique because its ending states a moral.

The beginning of a fable is brief and often launches right into descriptions of the characters and their actions. The time and setting are sometimes told, but are always vague and unimportant. For instance, time might be "one day" or "one very warm summer," and setting might be described as "walking through the jungle" or "returning from the pasture."

A fable's setting is also a backdrop, irrelevant to the characters or to the problem. Characters in a fable are usually personified animals. They are presented stereotypically: an owl is wise, a cat is curious. Characters are also flat, so we do not know the characters in any depth. The author uses dialogue to carry the action and create personification.

Plot is usually a person–against–person conflict, or in the case of a fable, personified animals against other personified animals.

The story's conflict is connected to the moral and is one–dimensional. The characters' actions to solve the conflict are usually accomplished in one or two episodes or events. A fable's resolution must lead us to a life lesson or moral at the tale's end.

Variety Within the Genre

There are three main collections of fables: Aesop's Fables, The Panchatantra, and the fables of La Fontaine.

Aesop's Fables: There is some debate about the person behind the name, but many agree Aesop was a former slave who lived about 3,000 years ago in Greece. He became well-known for his clever animal fables, and because of his intelligence and wit, he was given his freedom by his master. Aesop never wrote down his fables, so not until 200 years after his death did the first collection of his fables appear translated into Latin. They later were translated into English, French, and German. Sutherland (1997) considers Aesop's Fables as the purest form of fable.

Panchatantra: The Fables of India are the oldest known collection of Indian fables. *Panchatantra* means "five formulas" and is actually a textbook on wise conduct written around 200 B.C. The five sections are "Loss of Friends," "Winning of Friends," "Crows and Owls," "Loss of Grain," and "Ill-Considered Action." These fables are longer than Aesop's Fables and are written in verse, primarily for adults. They were translated into Latin and became popular in medieval Europe. The *Fables of Bidpai* is another version of the *Panchatantra*. The *Jatakas* are fables from India without a known author that originated in the 5th century or earlier. The *Jatakas* contain as many as 3,000 tales that teach lessons about using the intellect to solve or explain dilemmas, problems, or mysteries. They also stress the importance of moral conduct and good behavior. The *Jatakas* are written in a narrative form, but often give the morals in verse (Sutherland, 1997).

La Fontaine's fables: La Fontaine was a seventeenth-century French poet who translated Aesop's Fables into French and wrote many of his own fables. He wrote fables in verse, similar in style to Aesop's fables, though translations may change the fable to the prose form. LaFontaine was so popular that the French people called him "le fablier."

Today, fables appear in collections such as *Aesop's Fables* selected by Michael Hague; *Doctor Coyote: A Native American Aesop's Fable* (1987) by John Bierhorst; *The Dragon's Tale and Other Animal Fables of the Chinese Zodiac* (1996) by Demi; and *Fables* (1980) by Arnold Lobel. Fables can also appear alone: *Seven Blind Mice* (1992) by Ed Young; *Once a Mouse* (1961) by Marcia Brown; and *Town Mouse, Country Mouse* (1994) by Jan Brett.

Teaching the Fable

Read-Aloud Activities

To begin teaching about fables, hold a brainstorming session to find out what students already know about fables. Begin the brainstorming session by asking students to think of an experience they have had from which they have learned a lesson for life. Have students tell about their experiences, and encourage them to end with a short saying or moral that others could remember to avoid making the same mistake. After students have had an opportunity to share their experiences and lessons, tell them that storytellers often told short stories that would remind people how they should act. Explain that the life lesson is called a *moral*, and we often remember the moral even if we forget the fable. This discussion will lead into the Morals Meaning Quiz (see Figure 4.5).

To help students develop an understanding of the elements of fables, choose a story to read aloud to the whole class. Since fables are short, you may want to share two or three for background knowledge of this subgenre before working through the teaching techniques. Because Aesop's fables are so well-known, it might be best to begin with these. While reading aloud, you will demonstrate and apply the elements.

Figure 4.5   Morals Meaning Quiz

Here are some famous morals. Can you give either the fable it came from or what you think the moral means?

1. Slow and steady wins the race.
2. Look before you leap.
3. Beauty is only skin deep.
4. People are judged by the company they keep.
5. Do not count your chickens before they are hatched.
6. A simple life in peace and quiet is better than a luxurious life tortured by fear.
7. Little friends may prove to be great friends.
8. It is easy to be brave when you are far away from danger.

Answer: 1. The Hare and the Tortoise; 2. The Fox and the Goat; 3. The Leopard and the Fox; 4. The Husbandman and the Stork; 5. The Milkmaid and her Pail; 6. The Town Mouse and the Country Mouse; 7. The Lion and the Mouse; 8. The Wolf and the Kid.

The fable that will be modeled in this unit is an Aesop fable called "The Lion and the Mouse" that is found in Michael Hague's book *Aesop's Fables* (1999). It is an appropriate read–aloud for intermediate grades, and all activities and questions used in this unit are suitable for most fables. Therefore, choose fables that you like that are appropriate for your grade level. (See the bibliography of fables on page 166 for additional possibilities).

Comprehending Time and Setting

A fable's beginning is very brief. As stated previously, occasionally the time of the tale is given, but often it remains rather vague. If the fable is illustrated, the pictures may show the time of the tale. In our read–aloud, the time of the tale is not mentioned, but Hague's illustration shows it to be either early in the day or early evening.

In "The Lion and the Mouse," the first setting is the lion's lair and the second is the forest. This will illustrate to students that the setting of a fable is usually a backdrop:

> "A mighty lion was sleeping in his lair when he was awakened by a tiny mouse…" (p. 5).
>
> "Despite his great strength, the Lion could not break free. Soon the forest echoed with angry roars" (p. 5).

Identifying Types of Characters

The characters in a fable are animals who are personified and portrayed stereotypically. There are usually one or two main characters in a fable, and not many others. These questions and activities will help students identify the personified characters and their traits:

1. Who are the characters in this fable?
2. Do these animals have the characteristics you expected them to have?

In our read–aloud, there are two main characters: Lion and Mouse. To help students understand the stereotypic characteristics or traits of animals, have them brainstorm to make a chart of animals and their characteristics. Ask students to name animals, then fill in the animals' characteristics, or you could list some of the traits of animals that are common in fables and have students fill in the animal names. (Character traits could include shy, vain, brave, strong, slow, weak, fast, clever, wise, busy, proud, and greedy.) Students must be able to justify their answers before placing the animals in these categories.

Following the Plot

Use the questions and activities in this section to help students follow the quick introduction of the story action to the quick resolution and moral of the fable.

1. Do the characteristics of the animals determine the action of the story?
2. Is there one event in the fable or more? What are the events?
3. What is the resolution to the fable?
4. How do the problem and resolution lead us to the moral of the fable?

In our read–aloud, Lion, who is king of the forest, lets the mouse go because he is amused by the idea that a mouse might be able to repay him for sparing the mouse's life. Mouse is weak but very brave, and later he saves Lion's life.

The fable "The Lion and the Mouse" has two events. The first is Mouse's capture and release, and the second is Mouse's return to save Lion's life. The resolution of this fable is a speech by Mouse, in which we learn the moral:

"There!" said the Mouse proudly, "You laughed at me when I promised to repay your kindness, but now you know that even a tiny mouse can help a mighty Lion." (p. 5)

A Fable Map (see Figure 4. 6) may help students see the whole structure of a fable.

Understanding the Author's Style

Remind students that characters in fables are portrayed by personified animals, which means that the animals speak and act like human beings. In the text we see that these animals can speak like humans. In our read-aloud, both Mouse and Lion hold conversations. Animals also may be portrayed wearing clothes. In Hague's illustration for "The Lion and the Mouse," Lion is wearing a purple cape and wears a crown on his head; Mouse is dressed in a jacket and a scarf.

Figure 4.6   Fable Map

"The Lion and the Mouse"

Simple beginning (may include time and setting)	Lion's lair Forest
One or two characters (may have opposite characteristics)	Mouse who is weak and timid Lion who is strong and mighty
Problem	Episode One: Mouse is going to be eaten by Lion.
One or two events to solve the problem	But he is spared by Lion because Mouse says he may be able to repay Lion.
Problem	Episode Two: Lion is caught in a hunter's net.
One or two events to solve the problem	Mouse gnaws the ropes and sets Lion free
Resolution which leads to moral	Mouse reminds Lion that even small friends can be a help to those who are mighty.
Moral	Little friends may prove to be great friends.

Authors craft a fable by showing much of the action through dialogue. Many times an author begins the fable with dialogue, which allows the reader to quickly meet the characters and get drawn into the action. To help students better understand the importance of dialogue in a fable, ask students to take the parts of the animals and read the story's dialogue as a script, while you narrate the rest of the story.

Small-Group Guided Reading

Give students the opportunity to read and explore other fables. The questions and instructional activities you shared during the read–aloud can be used with the small–group guided reading.

Encourage students to add their own questions to the list of questions used during the read–aloud. During this group time, have students choose fables to read and keep track of character traits and morals. Let them decide if one of the fables they read can be mapped on the Fable Map.

Questions for Small-Group Guided Reading of Fables

1. How did your group decide on the questions and activities you would use? Did your choices help you understand fables?
2. Who were the main characters and who were the supporting characters in the fable your group read?
3. Did the main character's traits affect the action of the fable?
4. How did the resolution lead to the moral?
5. What was the moral?

Independent Writing of Fables

Students will see the whole structure of the fable when they write their own fables using prewriting, drafting, revising, editing, and publishing activities. First, allow students to write their own moral or to choose a moral from a list. As students plan the writing of their fable, encourage them to use the Fable Map for Writing to help them plan their tale (see Figure 4.7). They can use the Fable Map as a guide as they fill in the details and write their stories.

Figure 4.7   Sam's Fable Map for Writing

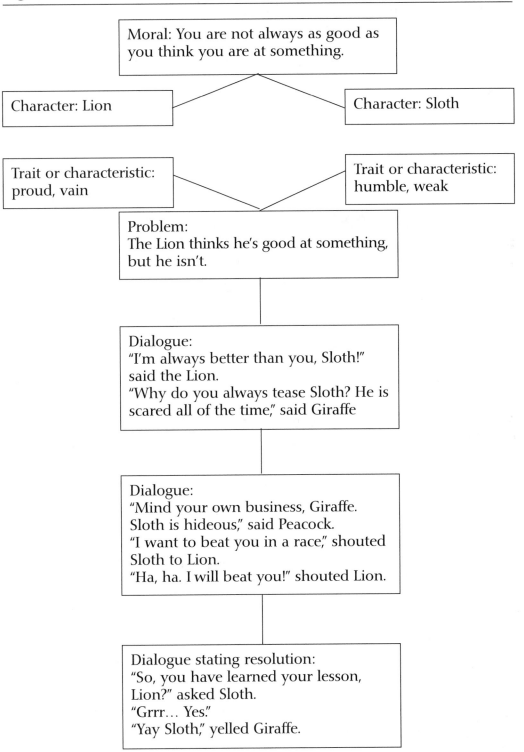

Moral: You are not always as good as you think you are at something.

Character: Lion

Character: Sloth

Trait or characteristic: proud, vain

Trait or characteristic: humble, weak

Problem:
The Lion thinks he's good at something, but he isn't.

Dialogue:
"I'm always better than you, Sloth!" said the Lion.
"Why do you always tease Sloth? He is scared all of the time," said Giraffe

Dialogue:
"Mind your own business, Giraffe. Sloth is hideous," said Peacock.
"I want to beat you in a race," shouted Sloth to Lion.
"Ha, ha. I will beat you!" shouted Lion.

Dialogue stating resolution:
"So, you have learned your lesson, Lion?" asked Sloth.
"Grrr... Yes."
"Yay Sloth," yelled Giraffe.

One fifth-grade student, Sam, brainstormed some morals that he thought might make a good fable. He then filled in the Fable Map for Writing and used peer discussions to develop his map. Sam drafted his fable after completing the Fable Map for Writing.

King Lion and Sloth in Wumbo Jumbo Jungle
by Sam

In Wumbo Jumbo Jungle, the King of the Jungle, Lion, always beat Sloth at everything.

"I am always better than you, Sloth!" yelled Lion.

The Sloth sighed. "Stop teasing Sloth, Lion! He is always scared anyway!" yelled Sloth's wife, Giraffe.

"Lion, I challenge you to a race!" the Sloth said proudly.

"Ha, ha, ha! I will beat you!" yelled Lion.

Well the day finally came, and the race was about to start. "Go Sloth," yelled Giraffe.

"Lion, you better not use too much energy now, you have to run to the supermarket later!" yelled Peacock.

"Ready..." Lion started.

"Say go!" said Sloth.

"Go!"

The Sloth started running but ran on to a tree. He was taking a shortcut!

Sloth won the race because of the shortcut, and Lion took a nap in the middle.

"So have you learned your lesson?" asked Sloth, now King of Wumbo Jumbo Jungle.

"Grrr...Yes," said the Lion.

"I knew you could do it!" yelled Giraffe.

Moral: You are not always as good as you think you are at something.

Questions for Writing Fables

This assessment gives students an opportunity to reflect on the process of writing a fable following the Fable Map. The questions ask students to provide a rationale for their choices of moral, characters and traits, use of dialogue, and a resolution which leads directly to the moral.

 1. How did you choose the moral for your fable? Did you choose a moral from a book or one from your imagination?

2. How did you choose your character traits? Were they appropriate for your moral?

3. How did you use dialogue to move the story along?

4. Does your resolution lead directly to your moral?

Pourquoi Stories and Fables Extensions

Culminate the Pourquoi Stories and Fables Unit with either a puppet show or a Readers Theatre presentation. (See Chapter Three, Traditional Folktale Extensions on page 76, for how to prepare a Readers Theatre.) Arnold Lobel's book *Fables* (1980) is particularly suited to Readers Theatre.

Read several fables or several pourquoi stories that portray the same animal. Compare the traits and problems of this animal. Are they the same in each story? Does the animal change when the tale is from a different country?

Now share the same fable from different collections. Does the fable remain the same? What could have caused differences?

Students could design a Storytelling Cube. The Plot Cube that was used as a prewriting activity in Chapter Three (page 73) could be used for this activity. On each square of the cube, have students write the name of either a fable or a pourquoi story. Then toss the cube and ask students to retell orally the story on the square that faces up.

Summary

Teaching the traditional literature of pourquoi stories and fables focuses on building an understanding of important literary elements. In pourquoi stories, students learn the elements of a patterned beginning, main and supporting characters, posing a question, and answering this question. The main concept behind a pourquoi story is describing the world as it used to be and how it is now.

In fables, students learn important elements such as personified, stereotypic characters; character traits; and a resolution that leads directly to a moral or life lesson.

To help students move from the genre of traditional literature to fantasy, we have included a unit on modern folktales. Modern folktales follow the same narrative text structure as traditional tales and incorporate some of the literary elements of fantasy.

Chapter Five

Teaching Modern Folktales

A subgenre of fantasy, modern folktales are enjoyable for students who are familiar with the traditional tales because these new stories, the modern slapstick versions of the old stories, follow the same format as our favorite folktales. Teaching modern folktales allows for a nice transition from traditional folktales, fables, and pourquoi stories to fantasy stories.

Background Information for Teachers

While this unit is intended for Grades 3 through 6, the beginning intermediate students will enjoy studying the same story structure used in the traditional folktale, and intermediate students will enjoy studying the ways that modern authors have changed traditional tales to fit our times. (See Figure 5.1, Elements by Level).

Figure 5.1   Elements by Level

Beginning Intermediate	Intermediate
Story Structure—literary folktale patterned beginning, setting, characters, problem, plot development	Story Structure—literary folktale patterned beginning, setting, characters, problem, plot development
Story Structure—spin-off setting, characters	Story Structure—spin-off setting, characters, point of view, language, plot, sequel
	Author's Style—motifs, patterned language, rhyme, figurative language

The study of modern folktales is a natural extension of the study of traditional folktales. However, these stories link to the genre of modern fantasy because they do have known authors. Tomlison and Lynch–Brown (1996) explain that the elements of traditional and modern folktales are very similar in that they both have "little character description, strong conflict, fast-moving plot with a sudden resolution, vague setting, and, in some cases, magical elements" (p. 127). Modern tales differ because they have a known, identifiable author who has modified the tale. In other words, modern folktales "do not spring from the cultural heritage of a group of people through the oral tradition but rather from the mind of one creator" (Tomlison & Lynch–Brown, 1996, p. 127).

Definition

Many authors attribute the first modern folktale to Hans Christian Andersen who published his first volume of stories in 1835. Hillman (1999) states that Andersen "blended successfully the two strains of modern fantasy and traditional folklore" (p. 141). Today authors not only write their own tales, but some authors have taken the liberty to twist the traditional tale in a modern and humorous way.

The modern folktale contains the same elements as the traditional story, and often the author writes a modern tale using the storyline from an old folktale. Huck, Helper, Hickman, and Kiefer (1997) state that "the story might be set in the days of kings and queens and beautiful princesses, the language will reflect the manners of the period, and the usual 'Once upon a time' beginning and 'They lived happily ever after' ending will be present—but the conflict usually has a modern twist" (p. 345).

Literary Elements of Modern Folktales

The story structure of the modern folktale follows the narrative structure of the traditional folktale, including a patterned beginning; vague setting; flat characters; one–dimensional conflict; an uncomplicated plot; actions of the main character to solve the conflict; and a quick, patterned ending.

The inclusion of the patterned beginning and the patterned ending have the same effect that these elements have in the traditional tale; the patterned beginning alerts the audience that the story will begin and that this story happened a long time ago, and the patterned ending alerts the audience that the story is over, just as it was during oral storytelling.

In the modern tale, the characters are flat and undeveloped and they are either good or bad. Characters also can include personified animals and objects. The setting is a backdrop setting, giving readers the impression that this story could take place in any toy room, forest, or castle. The conflict is simple and the character is involved in a fast-paced plot to solve this conflict. The middle of the tale includes the actions of the main character set off by an initiating event. The conflict is eventually resolved and the story ends quickly with a patterned ending.

Some authors have taken the traditional folktale and changed the story in some way to create a new story with a modern twist. These are called spin-offs, twisted tales, or fractured tales. Authors modernize the traditional tales by changing point of view, setting, characters, plot, or language, or by writing a new story to extend the existing one.

To illustrate to students how an author can change the story by changing the point of view, several stories could be shared: *Prince Cinders* by Babette Cole can be compared with "Cinderella," and *The True Story of the Three Little Pigs* by Jon Scieszka can be compared with "The Three Little Pigs." Discuss point of view and invite students to share how other familiar stories can be changed by telling the story from another view point. For example, students could tell "Cinderella" from the point of view of the stepsisters, or "The Three Billy Goats Gruff" tale from the troll's point of view.

Another way that modern-day authors reinvent the old stories is by changing the setting. Share with students that this can be accomplished with the illustrations or with the text. In her book *Somebody and the Three Blairs*, Marilyn Tolhurst changed the setting of the story by having the illustrator, Simone Abel, illustrate the book to show a modern-day home. Other examples in which the setting has been changed are *Hansel and Gretel* and *Jack and the Beanstalk* by Anthony Browne.

Characters in stories can also be changed. In Patricia Rae Wolff's *The Toll-Bridge Troll*, the author exchanges the three billy goats for a boy. Marilyn Tolhurst substitutes the three bears for three people in *Somebody and the Three Blairs*. Janet Perlman replaces the emperor with a penguin in *The Emperor Penguin's New Clothes* and Cinderella with a penguin in *Cinderella Penguin*. In the *Principal's New Clothes* by Stephanie Calmenson, the emperor is replaced by a principal.

Authors of modern folktales also use modern-day language in their books to add humor and to create an up-to-date version of the old story. In his book *Red Riding Hood*, James Marshall spruces up the language to sound current.

"Granny isn't feeling up to snuff today," she said, "so I've baked her favorite custard as a little surprise."

"Mama said not to speak to any strangers."

Marilyn Tolhurst also modernizes the language in *Somebody and the Three Blairs*:

"Somebody's been eating my Crunchies," said Mr. Blair.

"Somebody's been eating my Crispies," said Mrs. Blair.

"Somebody's been raiding the fridge," said Mrs. Blair.

"Naughty!" said Baby Blair.

Here is dialogue in Babette Cole's *Prince Cinders*:

"Rats!" said the fairy.

"Wrong again, but I'm sure it all wears off at midnight."

Changing the plot of the story can be fun and interesting, as is the case with Jane Yolen's *Sleeping Ugly*, a retelling of the traditional tale "Sleeping Beauty." In this tale, the author reverses the theme of the traditional tale by illustrating that inner beauty is far more important than physical beauty. *Sleeping Ugly* does not end with the main character living in a castle full of riches, but instead living with a family that is loving and caring. Authors also change the plot to create a modern-day story. *Snow White in New York* by Fiona French and *Prince Cinders* by Babette Cole are up-to-date versions of classic folktales that include discos, cars, buses, and modern dress.

Some authors have written sequels to old familiar folktales. Jon Scieszka's *The Frog Prince Continued* and Teresa Celsi's *The Fourth Little Pig* are excellent examples of sequels that you can share with students.

The theme of a modern folktale can mirror the theme of the traditional folktale where good overcomes evil. However, in modern tales good is not always rewarded and evil is not always punished because the theme does not reflect a cultural heritage.

Author's style in modern folktales includes patterned language, rhyme, and motifs to hold the reader's attention. The motifs found in the modern folktale are the same as those found in fantasy: magic, secondary worlds, good versus evil, heroism, special character types, and fantastic objects (Madsen, 1976).

Variety Within the Genre

There are two distinct types of modern folktales: the literary tale, which replicates the story structure of the traditional folktale but is written by a known author, and the spin-off, which changes some aspect of the traditional tale to modernize and update the story.

Literary folktales are stories in which the author uses the same literary elements as the traditional folktale. The quick flow of the written story emulates the style of a storyteller. While the traditional tale reflected the values of the storyteller's society or culture, however, authors of modern literary folktales allow their voices to come through in their tales. For example, some Hans Christian Andersen tales reflect his life, but Jane Yolen "writes lyrical tales that make use of modern psychological insights while following the traditional patterns in folk literature" (Huck et al., 1997, p. 345). Examples include Andersen's "The Ugly Duckling," "The Princess and the Pea," and "The Steadfast Tin Soldier" (all found in *Twelve Tales* (1994), edited and translated by Erik Blegvad); James Thurber's *Many Moons* (1990); Jane Yolen's *The Emperor and the Kite* (1988) and *The Girl Who Loved the Wind* (1972); and Kenneth Grahame's *The Reluctant Dragon* (1983).

Spin-offs of traditional folktales are stories written by authors who take the original folktale and rewrite it by changing some aspect of the old tale. Some examples include Babette Cole's *Prince Cinders* (1987), James Marshall's *The Three Little Pigs* (1989), and Jon Scieszka's *The True Story of the Three Little Pigs* (1989).

Teaching the Modern Folktale

Read-Aloud Activities

To begin the unit on modern folktales, hold a brainstorming session on what students already know about this genre, and record the results on charts in the classroom. As students become more familiar with modern folktales, these charts can be revised and updated. To introduce students to different modern folktales, ask them to match the ti-

Figure 5.2 Modern Folktale Quiz

Match the title of the folktale to an episode in the folktale.

1. *The Girl Who Loved the Wind*	a. She sleeps on twenty mattresses.
2. *The Little Match Girl*	b. She wants the moon.
3. *The Emperor's New Clothes*	c. He has to fight King George.
4. *The Fir Tree*	d. A monk sings to her.
5. *The Reluctant Dragon*	e. A wise blind man helps her.
6. *The Princess and the Pea*	f. He is rejected by a ballerina.
7. *The Steadfast Tin Soldier*	g. She is protected by a high wall.
8. *Many Moons*	h. She carries an old apron.
9. *The Emperor and the Kite*	i. He wanted to be big.
10. *The Seeing Stick*	j. He has to have new clothes.

Answers: 1–g, 2–h, 3–j, 4–i, 5–c, 6–a, 7–f, 8–b, 9–d, 10–e.

tle of a modern folktale with one of its episodes (see Figure 5.2). If students are not familiar with these literary or modern folktales, invite them to read the stories. (See page 166 of the bibliography for more modern folktales to share.)

Select books for a whole–class read–aloud that will help students to develop an understanding of the elements of modern folktales. While reading these books, demonstrate and apply the elements through teaching strategies. Design the following charts prior to the read–aloud: Comparing the Old & New Chart (page 104), Modern Folktale Map (page 105), Motif Chart (page 106), and Spin–Off Map (page 107).

Comparing the Old and the New

Use the following questions and activities to demonstrate the differences between a traditional folktale and a modern folktale. To begin this unit we will compare the traditional folktale *Cinderella* (1985) by Charles Perrault, as retold by Amy Ehlich, to the spin–off *Prince Cinders* (1987) by Babette Cole, but any modern folktale and its traditional counterpart can be used to illustrate this concept. After both stories have been shared, discuss the differences in the two stories by asking the following questions:

1. Who is the author of the modern tale?
2. How did the author change the traditional story?
3. How are the two tales the same? How are they different?

After you have discussed these questions, ask students to create a chart that compares the similarities and differences of the two stories. Older students can make these comparisons by drawing a Venn Diagram, while younger students should fill in a Comparing the Old and New Chart. The following Comparing the Old and the New Chart was designed by Bao, a third-grade student, after the stories were read in her class.

Comparing the Old and the New Chart

Cinderella (old)	Prince Cinders (new)
She went to the ball.	He went to a disco dance.
Her slipper fell off.	His pants fell off.
The Prince was kind of skinny.	The Princess was so skinny.
She had on a dress.	The Prince had pants on.
The king found a slipper.	The Princess found pants.
She goes to the ball in a carriage.	He goes to the disco in a car.
She had one stepmother and two stepsisters.	He had three brothers.
She had a girl fairy which she called her fairy godmother.	He had a boy fairy.
Her fairy godmother came down from the sky.	His fairy boy came down from the chimney.
She had her hair in a knot.	The prince had his hair in a ponytail.

This activity should lead to a discussion of who wrote the modern story and to an introduction of the terms *retold, translated, adapted by,* and *author.* Explain that *retold, adapted by,* and *translated* are associated with folktales that were first told orally and then written down by a collector because the original storyteller is unknown, while an author creates and writes a story from his or her imagination.

Comprehending the Modern Folktale

To help students comprehend the linear development of the modern folktale, ask the following questions and use the Modern Folktale Map found in Figure 5.3. The modern folktale that will be discussed in this section is Jane Yolen's *The Emperor and the Kite.*

1. What information does the author include in the patterned beginning?
2. Where does the story take place?

3. Who are the characters?

4. What is the conflict?

5. What is the event that starts the characters' action?

6. How does the character solve the conflict?

7. How does the story end?

To illustrate the quick beginning and the development of the story, create a Modern Folktale Map. Figure 5.3 shows the Modern Folktale Map for *The Emperor and the Kite*:

Figure 5.3   Modern Folktale Map

Patterned beginning: Once in ancient China

Setting: China

Characters: Djeow, monk, father

Problem: Evil men capture the emperor and take him to a tower.

Initiating event: Monk sings to Djeow each day. When the emperor is captured, he changes his song.

Next event: Djeow makes a string of grass, vines, and her black hair, and sends the rope up to the emperor.

Next event: The emperor slides down the rope.

Resolution: Djeow saves the emperor and is now noticed and loved by her father.

Patterned ending: "And the emperor never again neglected a person—whether great or small. And, too, it is said that Djeow Seow ruled after him, as gentle as the wind, and in her loyalty, as unyielding."

Understanding the Author's Style

Authors of modern day folktales use repetitive language and motifs, which are used to move the story along and to hold the audience's attention. Point out to students that these stories are written in a storytelling manner and ask them to pick out the special language the author uses. In this story Yolen starts the actions of the main character with a poem that is repeated as the monk passes the princess. When the emperor is captured, however, the poem changes because it is the monk's words in the poem that tell her how to solve the problem. Authors of modern folktales also use motifs. Since modern folktales are a subgenre of fantasy, alert students to the idea that the motifs found in these tales are also found in fantasy stories. Design a motif chart that students can use to identify the motifs in the read–aloud (see Figure 5.4 Motif Chart for *The Emperor and the Kite*).

Figure 5.4   Motif Chart for *The Emperor and the Kite*

Magic	Secondary World	Good v. Evil	Heroism	Special Character	Fantastic Objects
			X	X	X

Understanding the Spin-Off

To show students how the author changed the traditional tale into a spin–off, use the following questions.

1. Who is telling the spin–off story?
2. What is the title of the traditional tale?
3. How did the author change the setting?
4. Are the characters the same in both the traditional and the modern tale?
5. How did the author change the plot?
6. Did the author change the language?

To answer these questions, share examples of spin–offs and complete the Spin-Off Map. The Spin–Off Map will also show that some traditional stories are changed in several ways (see Figure 5.5). For example,

Figure 5.5   Spin-Off Map

Title	Point of View	Setting	Characters	Language	Plot	Sequel
Somebody and the Three Blairs		X	X	X	X	

Marilyn Tolhurst has changed the traditional story "Goldilocks and the Three Bears" with her story *Somebody and the Three Bears* (1994). In this spin–off, the author changes a number of things from the original tale–three bears are now three people; the Goldilocks character is now a bear called Somebody; the cottage in the woods is now a house in a city; porridge is now Crunchies and Crispies; and there are now five events instead of three. Therefore, to visualize the difference between the original tale and the modern spin–off, students can mark boxes on the Spin–Off Map for the elements of the original story that have changed.

Small-Group Guided Reading

Now give students the opportunity to read and explore modern folktales. Introduce books for small–group reading from the two categories of literary folktales and spin–offs. Let students decide which type of modern folktale they will read, then help them plan which strategies to use when reading their modern folktale. Also ask students to answer the questions and complete the activities that were used during the read–aloud during the small–group reading session.

While they are reading the modern folktales or the spin–offs, have students complete the following instructional activities: Comparing the Old and New Chart, a Literary Folktale Map, a Motif Map, and a Spin-Off Map.

Questions for Small-Group Guided Reading

Have students answer these questions in their guided reading groups:

1. What is the difference between a traditional tale and a modern folktale?
2. What is the difference between a modern literary folktale and a spin–off?

3. What were the motifs that the author included in the story your group read?

4. If the story you read was a spin–off, how did the author change this tale from the traditional tale?

Independent Writing of a Modern Folktale

Students should now be ready to write a literary folktale or a spin–off. Before they begin writing ask them to plan their tales by completing a Wordless Picture Book, a Plot Cube, or a Mapping a Modern Folktale, then choose strategies to develop their outline.

The Wordless Picture Book and the Plot Cube can be found in the unit on traditional folktales (see pages 72 and 73), and Mapping a Modern Folktale is introduced in Figure 5.6.

Students should now be ready to write a literary tale or a spin–off. Teachers of two third–grade classrooms taught the Traditional Folktale

Figure 5.6   Mapping a Modern Folktale

1. Decide what type of tale you will write, a literary folktale or a spin–off.
2. Decide where and when your story will take place.
3. Decide on at least three characters:
   a. the main character.
   b. the supporting character.
   c. a bad character.
4. If you are writing a literary tale, decide on one conflict for the main character.
5. If you are writing a spin–off, decide how you will change the original folktale.
6. Decide on the initiating event, which will start the action of the main character.
7. Decide on at least two other events that will follow the initiating event.
8. Decide on the motifs and how you will include them in your story.
9. Decide how to end your tale and write the patterned ending.
10. Design your story map:
    a. Beginning: patterned beginning, setting, characters, and conflict
    b. Middle: initiating event and two other events
    c. End: resolution and patterned ending
11. Write your tale.

unit first and then taught the Literary Folktale unit, and we will share some of their students' work. The first student, Heidi, wrote a literary folktale without using any of the prewriting activities that were suggested. She started with a draft and revised it for her published work.

The Princess's Rescue
by Heidi

Once upon a time in a far away land, there lived a king and his daughter. In the castle where they lived, they had servants, and among the servants there was a witch that disguised herself as a servant.

In another kingdom a prince and his father lived in another castle.

One night in the first castle while the princess rode her Magic Carpet up to her room, the witch that was disguised as a servant was waiting for her. As soon as the princess was in the room the princess was out with the witch. The witch took the princess to a dungeon and was going to leave her there with rats, bats, and an octopus with sixteen legs. While she was there the octopus pulled her under the water but she did not know how to swim. When she thought she was going to drown, a prince came and pulled her out of the water. Then he took her in his arms and they decided to get married.

Finally they got married in the princess's castle and they lived happily ever after.

Notice in Heidi's story that she included a patterned beginning, a setting, characters, a conflict, actions of the character, a resolution, and a patterned ending. She also included the motifs of magic—witch, patterned language, and a special character type (octopus).

Another third-grade student, Lindsay, wrote a spin-off of the traditional tale, "The Three Billy Goats Gruff," using the Wordless Picture Book as her prewriting activity.

The Three Trolls Truff
by Lindsay

There once lived three trolls in the woods. Their names were Orange Troll, Blue-Green Troll, and Pink Troll. There also was a big, mean billy goat called Big Billy Goat.

Then one day the mushroom patch that they lived in became empty because they ate them all. But they didn't want to go over the bridge even though there were the best tasting mushrooms on the other side.

"Squak, Squak, Squak" went Pink Troll, the tiniest troll. Big Billy Goat came out and Troll said, "I wanna go eat some mushrooms."

"Why should I let you cross?" said the Big Billy Goat.

"Because I'm the smallest and my bigger sister is still coming."

"OK. Fine. Go then." The troll wobbled into the mushroom patch.

"Honk, Honk, Honk," went Blue-Green Troll, the second biggest troll. Big Billy Goat came out and Blue-Green Troll said, "I wanna go eat some mushrooms."

"Why should I let you?" said Big Billy Goat.

"Because I wanna eat some mushrooms and my bigger brother is still coming."

"OK. Fine. Go then." The troll ambled over the bridge.

"Boom! Boom! Boom!" went Orange Troll, the biggest troll. Big Billy Goat came out and the troll said, "I wanna go eat some mushrooms."

"Why should I let you?" said Big Billy.

"Because I wanna go eat some mushrooms and my bigger brother is coming."

"OK. Fine. Go then." The troll stomped over the bridge into the mushroom patch.

Big Billy Goat waited and waited for the bigger troll. But it never came. When the three trolls came back, Orange Troll knocked Big Billy Goat off the bridge and they never saw him again.

And they lived happily ever after.

In her spin-off, Lindsay reverses and renames the characters, designs a new setting by including the mushroom patch, and uses her own repetitive language for the talking animals. She also incorporates the number 3 and the motif of trickery—all part of the original tale.

A third student, Katie, wrote a spin-off of "Beauty and the Beast." In her spin-off, she changes the characters, the setting, the conflict, and the events. She includes patterned language and the motifs of special character types, a magic object, and a transformation. She modernizes the story by including a library, the Internet, a television show, and books.

Beauty and the Lizard
by Katie

Once upon a time there was a very fair maiden named Beauty. Her father, who was a watch collector, told her to watch over the cottage until he got home from the library. When he left, a small lizard crept onto the window sill. Beauty saw this and threw a book at him. He responded by saying, "You're not as sweet as you seem." Beauty's face got so red with anger you would swear that she was going to explode. Suddenly she calmed down and spoke gently.

After a while her father came home and announced to her that the library was on fire. The small cottage was next to the library and soon caught on fire also. Beauty carried all sorts of things out of the cottage and away from the fire. Beauty ran into the forest carrying the lizard, followed by her father.

Beauty cried and cried. The lizard told her about a wonderful kingdom called Kizoodoo. Not believing, Beauty said that he might have seen it on the Net or on Nick-at-Nite. The lizard laughed and told her about a wicked fairy godmother and the spell.

The next day Leonardo De Vinci stopped by to show off his newest paintings, *The Moaning Jessie* and the *Groaning Chief*. He wanted to know what rhymes with "groaning" besides "moaning." Beauty, whose full name is Beauty Mona Lisa, got painted by Leonardo De Vinci. The painting was called the *Mona Lisa*. Her dad was also painted. This painting was called the *Billben*.

That night a fairy godmother flew into the house. The lizard awoke to see the fairy godmother look into the spell book to find a page. She found it and pointed her wand at the lizard and said, "Bibbitty, bobbity boo." The lizard turned into a handsome prince. Beauty woke up, saw him and they got married.

The end

Questions for Writing Modern Folktales

These questions give students the opportunity to reflect on the process of writing a modern folktale by asking for a rationale for their choice of type of modern folktale, theme, and changes included in their spin-off.

1. What was the message of the modern folktale that you wrote?

2. What motifs did you include in this tale?

3. If you wrote a spin-off, how did you change the traditional tale?

4. Would you like to share your modern folktale with others?

5. Will you write another modern folktale?

Modern Folktale Extensions

Students may enjoy finding out more about the authors of these modern tales, so obtain biographies, autobiographies, or author study resources to facilitate their study. For example, students might wish to read the biography by Joann Johansen Burch, *A Fairy Tale Life: A Story about Hans Christian Andersen*, or Jane Yolen's autobiography, *A Letter From Phoenix Farm*. (See page 171 of the bibliography for additional titles.)

Students might also enjoy working together to write a Zany Folktale. To write a Zany Folktale, tell them to choose three characters from three different folktales, such as the youngest billy goat, the pig that built the house of brick, and Cinderella. What will their problem be and how will they solve it?

As a class, students could write or tell a Collaborative Spin–Off of a traditional folktale. The class can decide which traditional tale they want to revise and, as a class, students will spin their tale. The first student or group of students begins the story, the next student or group of students adds on to the tale, and this continues until all of the students have participated and the story ends.

Another extension idea involves a group of students constructing a collage mural of a favorite folktale. Students can use any medium, or include real items from nature to create a scene. Texture can be added through the use of fabrics for clothing, yarn for hair, and crumpled blue tissue paper for lakes.

Summary

By studying modern folktales, students will gain an understanding of the differences between oral tradition and authorship when they compare traditional and modern folktales. Even though these tales contain the same backdrop settings, flat characters, and one–dimensional conflicts, modern folktales are the creations of the author and a subgenre of fantasy. Therefore, the motifs found in modern folktales are similar to those in fantasy, and the theme is entirely the creation of the author.

Because the modern folktale is a subgenre of fantasy, the next unit will discuss how to teach the structure and the elements of fantasy to young students.

Chapter Six

Teaching Fantasy

Fantasy is a popular genre with students of all ages because of its magical aspects, preposterous characters, and bizarre settings. Because so many classic fantasy stories have been made into movies, many students are familiar with this genre.

Background Information for Teachers

This unit can be customized by grade level depending on the students' abilities and their background knowledge of the genre (see Figure 6.1). Beginning intermediate students can study the basic elements of fantasy, and intermediate students can learn additional elements that will improve their reading and writing of fantasy.

Figure 6.1   Elements by Level

Beginning Intermediate	Intermediate
Variety	Variety
Story Structure	Story Structure
Setting—integral	Setting—real world, fantasy world moving from real to fantasy world
Characters—round, flat, fantastic	
Conflict	Characters—round, flat, fantastic
Plot Development—initiating event, subsequent events, resolution and end	Conflict
	Plot Development—initiating event, subsequent events, resolution and end
	Author's Style—motifs and personification

Definition

Tomlison and Lynch-Brown (1996) give us a simple yet useful definition of fantasy: "Modern fantasy refers to the body of literature in which the events, the settings, or the characters are outside the realm of possibility" (p. 121). Hickman and Cullinan (1989) remind us that the main problem facing authors of fantasy is that in these stories "the incredible and the impossible are made convincingly real" and "the new and the strange sit comfortably within a world that is believable, immediate, and authentic" (p. 110).

Some classify fantasy as either *low fantasy* or *high fantasy*. In low fantasy the story occurs in our world, but magical elements make the story impossible. In high fantasy the story takes place in a secondary world where rules are different from our world but remain consistent in the secondary world.

Many books in this genre continue characters and settings over many volumes, with trilogies appearing often. Lloyd Alexander and J.R.R. Tolkien are two authors who have written trilogies.

Looking through fantasy titles, students will realize they know many stories from movies. Titles such as *Charlotte's Web* (1952) by E.B. White, *The Adventures of Pinocchio* (1989) by Carlo Collodi, *Charlie and the Chocolate Factory* (1998) by Roald Dahl, and *Babe, The Gallant Pig* (1995) by Dick King-Smith were popular fantasy stories made into movies.

Literary Elements of Fantasy

Fantasy stories are written with a narrative structure. The beginning mentions the main character; the supporting characters; the main character's problem; and the setting, either the real world or fantasy world. The plot is developed as the events are presented and the main characters act to solve their problem. The fantasy story ends with some resolution to a conflict, usually with good overcoming evil.

Suspension of disbelief is an important element in fantasy. It is the way an author writes to make the story believable. One way authors suspend the reader's disbelief is to make the setting integral to the story, either beginning their story in the real world and then moving to a fantasy world, or beginning and ending their story in a fantasy world. Another way to suspend disbelief is by creating believable good and bad characters that are either round, flat, or fantastic.

Lukens (1999) states that "if setting is essential to our understanding, the writer must make the reader see, hear, touch, and perhaps even smell the setting" (p. 172). An integral setting is detailed and consistent to help the reader form visual images and to make the story believable. For example, in *James and the Giant Peach* (1996), the author takes the reader with James as he experiences three worlds. The author's descriptions fulfill the two criteria of incorporating details and moving from the real world into the fantasy world. The author describes the first world of James:

> Up until this time, he had had a happy life, living peacefully with his mother and father in a beautiful house beside the sea. There were always plenty of other children for him to play with, and there was the sandy beach for him to run about on, and the ocean to paddle in. It was the perfect life for a small boy. (p. 1)

He then whisks us to the second world of James with his aunts:

> They lived—Aunt Sponge, Aunt Spiker, and now James as well—in a queer ramshackle house on the top of a high hill in the south of England. The hill was so high that from almost anywhere in the garden James could look down and see for miles and miles across a marvelous landscape of woods and fields; and on a very clear day, if he looked in the right direction, he could see a tiny gray dot far away on the horizon, which was the house that he used to live in with his beloved mother and father. And just beyond that, he could see the ocean itself—a long thin streak of blackish–blue, like a line of ink, beneath the rim of the sky. (pp. 2–3)

The author makes it easier for us to accept the fantastic world by sharing just how miserable and lonely James is in his new home living with his aunts. We understand that anything would be better than where he is living. The Peach, however, is a wonderful, safe world for James:

> It was a large hole, the sort of thing an animal about the size of a fox might have made. James knelt down in front of it and poked his head and shoulders inside.
> He crawled in. He kept on crawling.
> This isn't just a hole, he thought excitedly. It's a tunnel!
> The tunnel was damp and murky, and all around him there was the curious bittersweet smell of fresh peach. The floor was soggy under his knees, the walls were wet and sticky, and peach juice was dripping from the ceiling. James opened his mouth and caught some of it on his tongue. It tasted delicious. (pp. 24–25)

Another example of an author beginning their story in the real world and then moving to the fantasy world is Lewis Carroll's *Alice's Adventures in Wonderland Through the Looking Glass.*

Other authors begin their story in the fantasy world and stay in that fantasy world throughout the story, which is another way to suspend disbelief. For example, A.A. Milne begins his story *Winnie the Pooh* (1961) with an introduction that tells how Pooh got his name.

> If you happen to have read another book about Christopher Robin, you may remember that he once had a swan (or the swan had Christopher Robin, I don't know which) and that he used to call this swan Pooh. That was a long time ago, and when we said good–bye, we took the name with us, as we didn't think the swan would want it anymore. Well, when Edward Bear said that he would like an exciting name all to himself, Christopher Robin said at once, without stopping to think, that he was Winnie–the–Pooh. And he was. So, as I have explained the Pooh part, I now will explain the rest of it. (p. vii)

In this story, the animals participate in the storytelling. Milne has taken us directly into the world of fantasy and keeps us there.

Fantasy characters are either very good or very bad; there do not seem to be any in–between personalities in fantasy stories. However, there are different types of characters in a fantasy story: round, flat, and fantastic.

The main character in a fantasy is usually a well–developed, complete, round character because when authors design characters that are believable, readers are more likely to suspend disbelief. Supporting characters can be flat or fantastic. Flat characters are not well–developed, and fantastic characters can be animals that talk and act like human beings, little people, or characters with extraordinary character traits.

The conflict in a fantasy is a real–world problem that sometimes is solved using fantastic or unordinary means. These are the motifs, which help the storyline move forward and aid in solving the problem. These recurring elements make fantasy different from realistic fiction. Madsen (1976) identified six basic motifs in fantasy: magic, secondary worlds, good versus evil, heroism, special character types, and fantastic objects. Some fantasy stories contain all six of the motifs, for instance, *The Wonderful Wizard of Oz* (1996). A story containing all six motifs is considered high fantasy.

Plot development is the sequence of events leading to the resolution of a conflict or the solution of a problem. The resolution or ending is usually quick with good triumphing over evil.

Theme is the central idea developed in the story through the characters' actions, the settings, and the events of the plot. Themes are developed to include "universal struggles, values, and emotions" (Norton, 1995, p. 336). Serious themes can be developed in fantasy such as good over evil, love over hate, justice over tyranny, persistence over odds.

Personification is another literary element that authors use in fantasy to make special character types come alive. It is "the giving of human traits to nonhuman beings or inanimate objects" (Lukens, 1999, p. 199). Toys and animals can be personified in fantasy stories. Arnold Lobel is an expert at using personification in his *Frog and Toad* books.

Variety Within the Genre

Norton (1995) identifies eight types of stories within this genre, and within each story type there is great variety. We will discuss six of Norton's categories: articulate animals, toys that come alive, preposterous characters and situations, strange and curious worlds, little people, and time warps. Let's look at each category briefly.

Articulate animal stories, favorites within this genre, center on animals that talk but retain some of their animal characteristics. Some titles in this category include *The Cricket in Times Square* (1996) by George Seldon, *Runaway Ralph* (1991) by Beverly Cleary, *Bunnicula: A Rabbit Tale of Mystery* (1983) by Deborah and James Howe, and *Watership Down* (1997) by Richard Adams.

Toys that come alive stories are told from a toy's point of view. Some books in which authors give human characteristics to toys are *A Bear Called Paddington* (1960) by Michael Bond, *The House At Pooh Corner* (1956) by A.A. Milne, and *The Adventures of Pinocchio* (1989) by Carlo Collodi.

Preposterous characters and situations appeal to a child's sense of humor and love of exaggeration. Some titles include *James and the Giant Peach* (1996) by Roald Dahl, *Tuck Everlasting* (1985) by Natalie Babbitt, *Mary Poppins* (1962) by Pamela Travers, and *Mr. Popper's Penguins* (1992) by Richard and Florence Atwater.

Strange and curious worlds stories take place in worlds that are believable and authentic no matter how improbable the events become. The world must have its own laws and limits that are consistent. Some titles within this category include *Alice's Adventures in Wonderland Through the Looking Glass* (1992) by Lewis Carroll, *Peter Pan* (1950) by Sir James Matthew Barrie, and *The Lion, The Witch, and the Wardrobe* (1997) by C.S. Lewis.

Little people stories feature characters who are little people who live in a well-developed world of their own, with the story told from their point of view. Some titles in this category include *The Borrowers* (1953) by Mary Norton, *Gulliver's Travels* (1997) by Jonathan Swift, and *The Gammage Cup* (1990) by Carol Kendall.

Time warp stories encompass travels back in time and into the future. Favorites include *A Wrinkle in Time* (1962) by Madeleine L'Engle, *A Girl Called Boy* (1982) by Belinda Hurmence, *Devil's Arithmetic* (1990) by Jane Yolen, and *Red Hart Magic* (1985) by Andre Norton.

Teaching the Fantasy Story

Read-Aloud Activities

To begin the unit on fantasy, brainstorm with students to learn what they already know about this genre, and record the results on charts in the classroom. As students become familiar with the fantasy genre, these charts can be revised and updated. To help students understand the subtopics of fantasy, ask them to categorize on a chart titles of a variety of fantasy stories, in books and on film. A discussion of their favorite fantasy stories will help them to match the fantasy synopsis with its correct title in this fantasy preview (see Figure 6.2).

To demonstrate and apply the elements of fantasy, select a book to read aloud to the whole class. The following charts can be designed prior to the read-aloud: Integral Settings Chart (page 121), Round Character Chart (page 123), Real World and Fantasy World Plot Map (page 124), and the Motif Chart (page 125). While students listen to the fantasy, they will collect information to place on these charts. The number of chapters you share in one session will depend on the students' attention and your class schedule.

The fantasy read-aloud discussed in this unit is *Charlie and the Chocolate Factory* (Dahl, 1998), which is particularly appropriate for third and fourth grades. However, all the activities shared in this unit are suitable for most fantasies and are appropriate for any grade level. (See page 168 of the bibliography for additional fantasy stories.)

Help students develop a deeper understanding of the elements of fantasy by modeling the story structure, theme, and author's style by using the read-aloud and asking the questions in this section.

Figure 6.2   Fantasy Preview

Match the story synopsis with the correct title.

1. A stuffed animal is left at the station.
2. A boy who doesn't want to grow up takes three children on a magical flight to another world.
3. A magical nanny comes to a family. This nanny has an umbrella and can fly.
4. A boy finds a winning ticket in a candy bar that allows him to visit a magical factory.
5. A puppet becomes "a real live boy."
6. A mouse takes credit for inventions we thought a human invented.
7. Christopher Robin's toys come alive in Hundred Acres Wood.
8. On Christmas Eve, her toy comes to life and takes her to a magical world filled with music, candy, flowers, and dancing.

a. *The Adventures of Pinocchio*	e. *A Bear Called Paddington*
b. *Mary Poppins*	f. *Peter Pan*
c. *Ben and Me*	g. *Charlie and the Chocolate Factory*
d. *Winnie the Pooh*	h. *The Nutcracker*

Answers: 1–e, 2–f , 3–b, 4–g, 5–a, 6–c, 7–d, 8–h.

Setting the Stage for Fantasy

Fantasy authors usually build the reader's background knowledge about the character and the character's situation before taking us into the story. This is where we learn about the main character, the supporting characters, the world in which they live (be it real or fantasy), and the main character's problem. The following questions will direct the students' attention to this background information for any fantasy.

1. What does the author share about the main character at the beginning of the story?
2. How would you describe the main character's life in the beginning of the story?

Evaluating Setting

The questions and activity in this section will help students understand the importance of both a real world and a fantasy world in a story. If both the real world and the fantasy world are included in the story, both worlds must be fully discussed. The following questions about setting can be asked about any fantasy:

1. Does the story begin in the real world or the fantasy world?
2. How does the weather, time of day, or the season affect the character?
3. Does the author describe the setting using enough detail so that you believe it could be real?
4. If the author begins the story in the real world, how does the character get to the fantasy world?

Dahl begins *Charlie and the Chocolate Factory* in the real world at Charlie Buckett's home at the edge of town. In this story, the season is winter and the weather is very cold, making the Bucketts' home very uncomfortable.

Ask students to write down attributes of the settings found in the fantasy you are sharing. In *Charlie and the Chocolate Factory*, there are two settings: the real world setting (the Bucketts' home) and the fantasy setting (Willy Wonka's Chocolate Factory). Both settings are well developed. The attributes of the Bucketts' home include cold drafts, smells of cooking cabbage and potatoes, two rooms with seven people, and one bed for all to sleep in. The attributes for the factory include warmth, roar of machines, sounds of a waterfall, and smells of hazelnuts and apple blossoms. To illustrate the dramatic differences between the two worlds, construct an Integral Settings Chart (see Figure 6.3).

Finally, the main character moves from the real world to the fantasy world when he discovers the ticket. When Charlie finds the Golden Ticket in his Wonka Bar, he is permitted to tour the chocolate factory. (For your fantasy read–aloud the answer to how the character discovers the fantasy world may be different.)

Identifying Characters

The questions and activities in this section will help students identify the types of characters (round, flat, and fantastic) found in fantasy stories. The type of characters in a fantasy story depends on what the author wants to achieve in the story. Characters usually are very good or very bad. Either way, they must be believable and consistent. These basic questions about characters can be used for any fantasy:

1. Who are the characters in the story?
2. Which characters are round and fully developed?

3. Which characters are flat?

4. Are there fantastic characters in this story?

The story's characters may be the same in the real world and the fantasy world, or there may be different characters in the two settings. Construct a list of the characters in the story with your students. There are 12 characters in *Charlie and the Chocolate Factory*: Mr. and Mrs. Buckett, Grandpa Joe, Grandma Josephine, Grandpa George, and Grandma Georgina are the characters in the real world; and when Charlie and Grandpa Joe enter the fantasy world, they meet Augustus Gloop, Veruca Salt, Violet Beauregarde, Mike Teavee, Mr. Willy Wonka and his helpers, the Oompa–Loompas.

Figure 6.3   Integral Settings Chart

	The Real World The Bucketts' Home	**The Fantasy World** The Chocolate Factory
Feels	jets of freezing air icy	nice and warm inside
Sounds	cold drafts blowing	clanking and sputtering waterfall suck–suck–sucking sounds
Smells	smell of cabbage, potatoes and bread cooking	marvelous smells of coffee, burnt sugar, hazelnuts and apple blossoms
Tastes	cabbage, bread, potatoes	minty grass and buttercups chocolate, fantastic
Looks	two rooms, one bed, mattresses on the floor, old people huddled together	large shiny metal door great brownish muddy river enormous pipes butter cups, grasses, rivers, underground tunnels

Now list the attributes of all the 12 characters and analyze them to determine which characters are fully developed and which characters are flat. In our read–aloud, the round characters are Charlie and Willy Wonka. Design a Round Character Chart (Figure 6.4) to show the attributes of these two characters. The flat characters are the other children Charlie meets in the factory (Augustus Gloop, Veruca Salt, Violet Beauregarde, and Mike Teavee) and Charlie's family members (Mr. and Mrs. Buckett, Grandpa Joe, Grandma Josephine, Grandpa George, and Grandma Georgina).

Question 4 asks students to identify any fantastic characters: The Oompa–Loompas are extraordinary in *Charlie and the Chocolate Factory*.

Plot Development

The questions and activities in this section help students follow the initial event, the subsequent events, and the actions of the characters. Pose the following questions to demonstrate the development of the plot for any fantasy:

1. What does the author share at the beginning of the story about the character?
2. What is the initiating event?
3. What are the other events that move the story along?
4. How does the author move the main character into the fantasy world? (if applicable to your read–aloud)
5. What motifs did the author use in the story?

Using the Real World and Fantasy World Plot Map in Figure 6.5 (see page 124), students can identify the real world, the fantasy world, and the events that occurred in both.

Understanding the Author's Style

The questions and activity in this section will help students understand the literary elements that authors use in fantasy, personification, and motifs. The following questions can be asked when discussing author's style:

1. Did the author use personification?
2. Did the author include any motifs?

Figure 6.4   Round Character Chart

Charlie	Mr. Willy Wonka
Appearance Small boy, skeleton—thin face Frightening white with pinched skin drawn tight	**Appearance** Little man, black top hat, plum-colored tail coat
Actions Sleeps in room with parents Walks past the factory on way to and from school Loves chocolate Lifts small pointed nose to smell chocolate Walks slowly Listens to Grandparents tell stories	**Actions** Quick, jerky little movements with head like a squirrel Quickness of movements Skipping dance— "turned right, turned left, he turned right again"
Speech "Oh, it's wonderful!"	**Speech** "Welcome, my little friends! Welcome to the factory!" Voice high and fluttery "Please go in!"
Thoughts Made changes to life to save energy Loves chocolate	**Thoughts** Loves factory Thinking of future of factory
What Others Say "He's a fine fellow." "He's beginning to look like a skeleton." "Why hasn't he got a coat on?"	**What Others Say** "He's gone off his rocker!" "He's crazy!" "He's balmy!" "He's nutty!"

Personification is a literary element that is often used in fantasy. The author of *Charlie and the Chocolate Factory* does not use personification, but other fantasy stories do contain personified animals and toys. If you are sharing books from the articulate animals category, tales where toys come alive, or stories set in strange and curious worlds, then students will easily grasp the concept of personification.

Now examine, the motifs used in *Charlie and the Chocolate Factory*. In the real world, readers learn of the special character—Mr. Willy Wonka—and about the secondary world that we will enter—The Chocolate Factory—and hear stories of no one being allowed to enter or leave the factory. Therefore, when we finally enter this secondary world, we are ready for the little characters, the fantastic setting, and

Figure 6.5   Real World and Fantasy World Plot Map

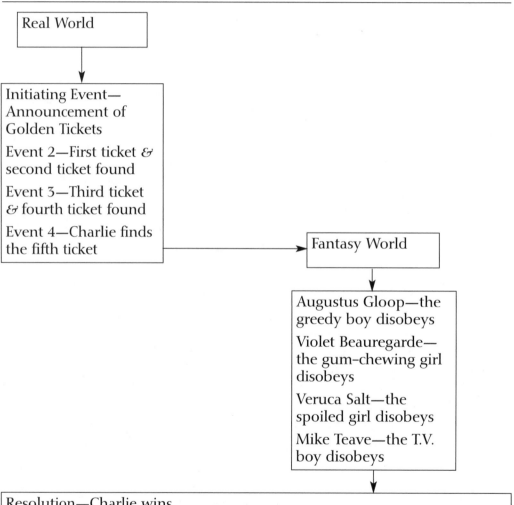

Real World

Initiating Event—Announcement of Golden Tickets

Event 2—First ticket & second ticket found

Event 3—Third ticket & fourth ticket found

Event 4—Charlie finds the fifth ticket

Fantasy World

Augustus Gloop—the greedy boy disobeys

Violet Beauregarde—the gum–chewing girl disobeys

Veruca Salt—the spoiled girl disobeys

Mike Teave—the T.V. boy disobeys

Resolution—Charlie wins.
End—Charlie inherits the chocolate factory, which becomes Charlie's new home.

Figure 6.6   Motif Chart

Story: *Charlie and the Chocolate Factory*

Magic	Secondary World	Good vs. Evil	Heroism	Special Character	Fantastic Objects
	X	X	X	X	X

the strange objects found in the factory. Use the Motif Chart (Figure 6.6) to examine the motifs found in a fantasy. The example has been completed for our read–aloud.

The climax occurs when the main character learns to solve his or her problem, and in the resolution, all the loose ends are tied together. The actual ending is brief. Questions to pose while discussing the ending of the story might include

1. When does the main character see how his or her problem could be solved?
2. How did you feel about the ending of the story?
3. Do you know what happens to the main character at the end of the story?
4. Who were your favorite characters in the story and why?
5. Do you feel that this story could really happen? How did you know it was a fantasy?

Small-Group Guided Reading

Now give students the opportunity to read and explore other fantasy stories. You can use the questions and instructional activities shared during the read–aloud during the small–group guided reading of fantasy stories.

Before they begin reading, ask students to plan questions to answer with their groups during reading. They can also work with you to plan which strategies to use for guiding their reading. Students may choose to fill in charts that they found useful during the class read–aloud. Also encourage students to add to the list of questions they answered during the class read–aloud.

Questions for Small-Group Guided Reading

Ask students these questions in their groups:

1. How did you decide on which questions and activities to use? Were your questions and activities effective in helping you understand fantasies?

2. Did the fantasy you read begin and end in the same setting? When were you aware of a fantasy setting?

3. Who were the characters in the real world and in the fantasy world? Which were round, flat, and fantastic?

4. What was the conflict in the story?

5. How did the main character solve the conflict?

6. What motifs did the author include in the story?

Independent Writing of Fantasy Stories

An effective way to help students see the whole structure of this genre is to have them write their own fantasy. To help students organize their story, instruct them to complete a Mapping a Fantasy Outline. Then allow students to choose strategies to develop their outline, which allows students to create a cast of characters and a story line before they begin their first draft. Figure 6.7 is an outline specifically designed for fantasy stories.

Now students can start a draft for their fantasy story.

When this unit was taught in a fifth–grade classroom, Brian incorporated a real–world setting and a fantasy setting. He also used the fantasy motifs of magic, special people, and fantastic objects. Brian used magazine pictures to design his fantasy world and then used these descriptions to make his setting integral to the story (see page 130 for Brian's Integral Setting Ideas).

After they have completed an outline, students can write their first draft. They may wish to get feedback from their peers after writing their draft. Then they can continue to write, revising for meaning and fantasy elements. When they are pleased with their fantasy, peers and teachers may help with the editing, and then the story is ready to publish.

Figure 6.7 Mapping a Fantasy Outline

1. Decide where to begin your story—in the real world or the fantasy world.
2. Decide on at least four characters for your story:
   a. The main character (a round character)
   b. One supporting character
   c. Two flat characters
   d. One fantasy character
3. Design a Round Character Map for your main character.
4. Design a Settings Chart for the settings in both worlds.
5. Decide on the problem of the character.
6. Decide how the main character will move to the fantasy world.
7. Decide which motifs to include in your story.
8. Design the outline for your fantasy story.
   a. Beginning: characters, settings (real world and fantasy world), and the main character's problem
   b. Middle: the initiating event and subsequent events—when and how to move the main character into the fantasy world—the motifs that you will use
   c. End: how the problem of the main character will be resolved and how your fantasy will end

Brian designed his fantasy world, wrote his draft, and published his fantasy story.

The Candy World
by Brian

One day two kids, Billy and Ann were at their grandma's house up in her attic having a pillow fight.

They were laughing and having a good time, but Billy got tired and wanted to stop. They started walking around and they found some very weird things such as a book for making atomic candy for your enemies or gum that gives off flavor without chewing it. Just as they were going to open the weird book with all of the recipes, their grandma called up the stairs, "Time to eat."

Billy and Ann went down the stairs to go eat. After they got done eating they went back up the stairs to go look at the very weird book. They opened the book and started to read.

How To Make Atomic Candy For Your Enemies!
1 cup sugar
8 red hot peppers
10 red jalapenos
7 atomic fire balls
1 cup vinegar
Mash all ingredients up and then make batter into balls. Once batter is in balls, bake at 250 degrees for 33 minutes. Batter should make about 22 balls.

Billy and Ann both thought this candy would be very hot indeed. Throughout the night the kids continued to read the book of candy making. After about 2 hours of reading the kids finally saw all of the recipes, but when they got to the back of the book there was a little key placed in a little glass box. The kids quickly got a rock from outside and broke the little glass box. They took out the key and under it was a note. Ann quickly took out the note and read it out loud. It said

Dear Friends,
You are probably wondering what this key is for. Well I can tell you what it's for. It's to open a very special door up in the attic of this very house. Where is it, you say? Well I know where it is too. It's under the bed. There should be a little silver keyhole under a little green box. Put the key in and open the door and then jump through. I now have let you be in control of magic.
Good Luck!

Ann and Billy didn't wait. They ran right over to the bed and crawled under it. They then began to look for a green box. Ann found it. She quickly hit the box off the keyhole, took the key from Billy and put it in the silver keyhole like the note had told about. Then she kicked the door. It flew open. What they saw was swirling colors.

"What is it?" asked Billy.

"I think it's a portal and I think we should go in and check it out," said Ann.

"But Ann, it looks dangerous, I don't think we should go in."

Then a noise started up. It sounded like a teapot going off! The kids had to shout now to talk to each other.

"I don't know about you, but I'm going in there!" shouted Ann. Then without warning Billy, Ann jumped into the portal. Billy, scared without a companion, jumped into the portal too. It was a shock to both Ann and Billy when they landed in a lake of melted chocolate. They swam to the bank of the chocolate lake, and what they saw was amazing. What they saw was a world made of candy! Now Billy, who loved candy, couldn't help running out to this new world and eating some of its candy grass. He yelled with joy as he ate the grass. "It tastes like peppermint!"

"Hey, hey, hey, wait a minute," said Ann. "We don't even know where we are and you're eating grass."

"Oh all right, I'll stop. But as soon as we find out where we are I'm eating some buttercups," said Billy.

The kids began to search for someone who could tell them where they were. They called and searched for about an hour, but found no one. They did see a castle about a mile away. The kids began to walk towards the castle. Billy couldn't help himself and he ate some of the road. They walked and walked until they got to the castle.

When they got there they hit a huge door handle. Some little man made out of dough opened the door just a crack and asked the kids what they wanted.

"We're Billy and Ann and we found a key in a book and it opened a door, and we found the door and went in, and now we ended up here. We just wanted to know where we are," said Ann.

"Well, why didn't you say so?" said the little man. "Come in!"

Billy and Ann went in. They had hot chocolate and the little man made of dough told them where they were and something very special besides that. When they were done with their hot chocolate, the man asked them, "Do you know what you are in possession of?"

"No," said the kids.

"What you are in possession of is a candy world you are in."

"We are?" said the kids.

"Yes, you are."

Billy and Ann ran out of the castle and went back through the portal. When they got back they told Grandma everything. The kids had possession to this world, and whenever they wanted candy, all they had to do was go under the bed and through the door to the candy world.

Questions for Writing Fantasies

This part of the assessment gives students the opportunity to reflect on the process of writing a fantasy, by providing a rationale for their choice of settings, characters, and motifs.

1. Did you build an integral setting that was described in detail? Did you make your characters believable, even those that were fantastic?

2. Describe why you began your fantasy in the real world or in the fantasy world.

Picture of:

jar of cookies:
These cookies are going to be the size of me.

piece of candy:
These are going to
be rocks.

nutcracker sweets:
The road will be
made of this.

mints:
The grass tastes like these.

caramel candy:
This is going to be a bridge made of
caramel and chocolate.

bedroom:
I chose this because
the walls that they
live in belong to this
bedroom.

plate of cookies:
Leaves will look and taste like these.

mansion:
I chose this picture because this is the mansion
where they live. (They live in the walls.)

3. What was your favorite character to develop and why?

4. What motifs did you use in your fantasy?

5. Would you like to share your fantasy with others?

6. Will you write another fantasy story?

Fantasy Extensions

To extend the Fantasy Unit, have students draw a map of their fantasy world. Have them look at Tolkien's and Alexander's maps of their fantasy lands, found in the front of their books, which will help young authors suspend disbelief and create an integral setting.

Students could also make a mural of the fantasy world found in their read–aloud or guided–reading text. Or students may wish to present a play based on an event in the read–aloud or shared book.

Ask students to think about the future when they write their fantasy story. Have them invent an object that will change the future of the world, and write a fantasy story about the world after the invention.

Summary

This unit focused on the important elements of fantasy, including suspending a reader's disbelief by developing integral settings and believable characters that are round, flat, or fantastic. Another element that was discussed was the development of the plot, which follows the characters' actions in response to the initial event. A significant aspect of fantasy is how the author uses personification to give human characteristics to inanimate objects or non–human beings and the use of motifs to move the story into the fantasy world.

With the conclusion of this unit on fantasy, we leave narrative text and begin an exploration of informational (or expository) text with the study of biographies.

Chapter Seven

Teaching Biographies

Biographies are considered informational text. Learning about accomplishments, strengths, and weaknesses of others allows students also to learn about different periods in history. Huck, Hepler, Hickman, and Kiefer (1997) state that "biography often bridges the gap between historical fiction and informational books" (p. 552).

Background Information for Teachers

Figure 7.1 shows how the literary elements of biography can be customized for beginning intermediate and intermediate level of students.

Definition

In the early 17th through 19th centuries, biographies were written to be "tools for religious, political, or social education. Emulation of biographical heroes was considered desirable" (Norton, 1995, p. 646). Even into the 20th century, only heroes, not controversial subjects,

Figure 7.1 Elements by Level

Beginning Intermediate	Intermediate
Fiction and Nonfiction	Fiction and Nonfiction
Chronological Order	Chronological Order
Beginning a Biography	Beginning a Biography
Characters—round	Characters—round, dynamic
Setting	Setting
Author's Style—dialogue	Author's Style—dialogue, anecdotes, flashbacks, jackdraws
	Theme

were written about. However, in the 1960s and 1970s a new view of worthy candidates for biographies emerged. Ordinary people in extraordinary circumstances, women, people of color, and people whose lives might be considered controversial are now the subjects of biographies. The content of the biography also changed during this period. Earlier biographers may have omitted or distorted details in order to make the character one whom children could emulate. Now there is a more honest, accurate treatment of the biographical subject.

A biography is an account of a person's life that is written by someone else. Because biographies must be as accurate as possible, they are written by authors who research, read about, and talk to people who know or have known the subject. Tompkins (1994) states that in biographies "writers combine elements of expository text writing with narrative writing. Writers take information from a person's life—dates, places, events, and people—and weave the factual details and sometimes dialogue into an entertaining account that readers can relate to" (p. 153).

Literary Elements of Biographies

Biographies are written as expository text. Expository text is subject-oriented and contains facts and information with little dialogue (Tonjes, Wolpow, & Zintz, 1999). Although authors of expository text will incorporate aspects of narrative, biographies often are organized differently than narrative text. When Calkins (1994) was writing memoirs in the classroom, she called the organization of a memoir plot lines of our lives, which is a very appropriate way to describe how biographies are organized. Biographies include a series of events in a person's life presented in a chronological sequence. Authors include specific facts when they share these events so that the reader can gain a clear understanding of what really happened. These facts are substantiated by documented information that describes the achievements or contributions of the person.

Setting in a biography contains accurate descriptions of where the person lived, worked, and played. An authentic setting must contain images of the times and places of the person portrayed in the biography, and the setting supports the character.

Characterization is the most important element in biographies. Characters in biographies are real people who function in authentic ways. These characters are dynamic, which means they do not stay the same as their story progresses; they change like any human being changes with the passage of time. Usually the subjects of biographies are heroes or heroines, sports figures, explorers and scientists, artists and musicians, authors and composers. Recently, common folk doing uncommon things have become subjects of biographies. Characters in biographies must deal with the complex issues of living in society, working with others, and playing with others. Authors may develop round characters through dialogue, actions, what others say about the character, and anecdotes or short stories to build believable characters (Lukens, 1999).

Theme is the reason why an author is writing the biography. Authors of biographies identify a central theme or thread that runs through the subject's life. This central theme ties together the character, the activities of the character, and the setting, and through the theme the character's contributions become prominent. In a biography, this interpretation of the theme is the author's (Huck et al., 1997), and the "author walks a thin line between theme and bias " (p. 558). To realize the theme is to identify the accomplishments of a person's life. The themes of working hard and struggling for freedom, working together with brothers and sisters, and sharing talents with others are common themes that repeat throughout biographies.

Authors use different techniques to bring the subject of a biography to life and to make the subject's life interesting to the reader. Authors use anecdotes, flashbacks, dialogue, and jackdaws to help the reader fully understand the character. An anecdote is a short account of an event, or a personal note about the subject, usually shared to entertain the reader or to make the subject more real.

To fill in missing information, the author uses flashbacks. A flashback is a type of reminiscing in which either the author or the character tells of an event that happened in the past. With this technique, an author may start the biography at the moment of the action, then fill in the earlier events through flashbacks. Flashbacks may be long or short and may include anecdotes or dialogue.

A jackdaw, according to Huck et al. (1997), "comes from the British name for a relative of the crow that picks up brightly colored objects and carries them off to its nest" (p. 687). In the classroom, a jackdaw is a collection of items that represent a period in history. The biographical jackdaw is a collection of materials: photographs, maps, songs, cartoons, newspaper articles, advertisements, and diagrams that add to the reader's understanding of the time period and a character's achievements. The designing of a jackdaw should not be limited to the past.

Variety Within the Genre

Tomlison and Lynch–Brown (1996) help us to classify biographies in two ways: (1) by the degree of documentation that the author has used, and (2) by the degree of coverage the author has accomplished. Within these two classifications, biographies can be divided into a number of varieties:

Authentic biographies are well–documented and use only primary data, which includes letters, eyewitness accounts, diaries, and interviews of the subject. The author makes up no details. *And Then What Happened, Paul Revere* (1973), *Bully For You, Teddy Roosevelt* (1991) by Jean Fritz, and *The Wright Brothers: How They Invented the Airplane* (1991) by Russell Freedman are examples of authentic biographies. Fritz and Freedman are biographers who are well–known for extensive documentation in their authentic biographies.

Fictional biographies are accurately reported factual presentations, but the author invents dialogue. Nancy Smiler Levinson's biography of John Thompson in *Snowshoe Thompson* (1992) is an example of a fictional biography.

Biographical fiction accurately reports achievements of a person, but the author may invent the dialogue, secondary characters, and reconstruct the actions. *Ben and Me* (1988) by Robert Lawson is an example of biographical fiction.

Biographies are also classified by the amount of coverage their subject's life has received. Some biographers cover only certain parts of a person's life, whereas others cover a person's entire life.

Complete biographies attempt to cover a person's entire life. *The Story of Harriet Tubman: Conductor of the Underground Railroad* (1991) by Kate McMullan and *A Fairy-Tale Life: A Story About Hans Christian Andersen* (1994) by Joann Johansen Burch are examples of complete biographies.

Partial biographies attempt to cover a portion of the person's life. *Abe Lincoln's Hat* (1994) by Martha Brenner and *Bloomers!* (1993) by Rhoda Blumberg are examples of partial biographies.

Collected biographies are collections of life stories of more than one person. *Black Pioneers of Science and Invention* (1970) by Louis Haber and *Stories of Ten Remarkable Athletes* (1993) by Bill Littlefield are examples of collections of biographies.

Whether the person presented is living or whether the person lived during another period in history also can classify biographies.

Contemporary biographies are written about a living person or one who has lived during the author's lifetime. *The Story of Walt Disney, Maker of Magical Worlds* (1989) by Bernice Seldon and *Oh, The Places He Went: A Story About Dr. Seuss* (1994) by Maryann Weidt are considered biographies about contemporary figures.

Historical biographies are written about a person who lived during a different time period than the author. *The Story of Laura Ingalls Wilder, Pioneer Girl* (1992) by Megan Stine is considered a historical biography.

Teaching the Biography

Pre–Read-Aloud Activities

To begin the unit on biographies, brainstorm with students to find out what they already know about this genre. After the brainstorming session is complete, discuss the differences between fiction (narrative text) and nonfiction (informational text) to help students understand that biographies provide information. Explain that these two types of books are organized differently and that a biography is a factual account of a person's life, whereas the events and characters in a fiction story are made up by the author. Students can identify the differences between the two types of books by sharing two picture books. For example, compare the biography by Carole Green, *L. Frank Baum: Author of the Wonderful Wizard of Oz* (1995) to the realistic fiction story *Amazing Grace* (1991) by Mary Hoffman.

After these differences have been shared, use a Who's Who in Biographies quiz to begin the study of biographies (see Figure 7.2). If students do not know about these subjects, invite them to read biographies of these people.

During Read-Aloud Activities

Select a biography to read aloud to the whole class in order to demonstrate and apply the elements of biography. The following charts can be designed prior to the read–aloud: Lifeline (page 138), Stepping Stones of Accomplishments (page 139), the Round Character Chart (page 141) and the Biography Settings Chart (page 142).

The biography read–aloud for this unit is *The Story of Harriet Tubman: Conductor of the Underground Railroad* (1991) by Kate McMullan. It is ap-

Figure 7.2   Who's Who in Biographies?

Match the name on the right with the word or phrase that describes an aspect of that person's life.

1. a kite and a key	a. Steven Spielberg
2. *Little House on the Prairie*	b. Hans Christian Andersen
3. makes ground-breaking movies	c. Dr. Seuss
4. "I have a dream."	d. Laura Ingalls Wilder
5. Underground Railroad	e. Ben Franklin
6. wrote down folktales	f. Martin Luther King
7. *Cat in the Hat*	g. Harriet Tubman

Answers: 1–e; 2–d; 3–a; 4–f; 5–g; 6–b; 7–c.

propriate for fifth and sixth grades, but all of the activities shared in this unit are suitable for most biographies and grade levels, so any biography may be selected for the read-aloud. (See page 170 of the bibliography for additional titles of biographies.)

Comprehending Biographies

Students will want to continue reading if the author draws them into the story with an interesting lead or beginning. The following questions and excerpt will help students understand the importance of beginning a biography in a surprising or interesting way. The question that could be asked about the lead is, what does the author share in the beginning of the biography that makes you want to read further? For example, Kate McMullan begins the book *The Story of Harriet Tubman* with this passage:

> **Hired Out**
> Two small black children drew with sticks in the dirt in front of a ramshackle cabin. Their older sister, Minty, whose real name was Harriet Ross, watched them. She wished that she could play, too. But she had work to do. It was a warm fall day. The field hands who picked crops for Edward Brodas would be thirsty.
> She must carry water to them. Minty picked up the heavy water buckets. She had no time for play.
> It was 1827 in Dorchester County, Maryland, and Minty was six years old. (p. 1).

Figure 7.3   Lifeline of Minty

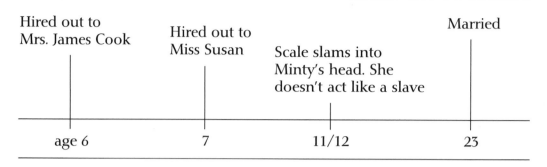

Following Lifelines

Students should be familiar with the concept of a timeline from their social studies classes. A timeline is a "visual display of the sequence of events from history" (Tompkins & McGee, 1993, p. 243); lifelines, on the other hand, "are a variation of timelines. Lifelines illustrate the accomplishments of a famous person or an ordinary person who has admirable qualities" (Tompkins & McGee, 1993, p. 243). To show students how authors organize the events in a person's life by using lifelines, ask the following questions and show Minty's lifeline.

1. At what point in the subject's life did the author begin this biography?
2. How did the author organize the passing of this person's life?

Introduce the concept of lifeline and as the read–aloud progresses, have students create the lifeline of the main character. A lifeline can be organized using events, age of person, or dates. The lifeline in Figure 7.3 is organized using Minty's age and a partial list of the events in her life. Lifelines can be creatively designed to reflect a person's life and accomplishments. (See the student poster lifelines of Walt Disney and Dr. Seuss in the Extensions section on pages 149 and 150.)

Understanding a Plot Line of Life

A biography is organized by placing events in a person's life in a chronological order, which is sometimes called a Plot Line of Life (Calkins, 1986). To help students gain an understanding of this type of organization, ask the following questions and show the Stepping Stones of Accomplishments chart in Figure 7.4.

? 1. What were the main accomplishments of this person?
2. How did these accomplishments affect other people?

   Where the biography begins is the author's choice. Our read–aloud biography is considered a full biography, even though the story begins when Harriet Tubman was 6 years old. Construct a Stepping Stones of Accomplishments chart to illustrate the accomplishments of the biography's subject. As the read–aloud is shared, have students compile a list of Harriet Tubman's accomplishments. The last stone lists all the accomplishments of the subject. A Stepping Stones of Accomplishments for Harriet Tubman might look like Figure 7.4.

Identifying Character Traits

   The questions and activities in this section will help students identify how an author describes the biography's subject as a round char-

Figure 7.4   Stepping Stones of Accomplishments for Harriet Tubman

acter who changes with the passage of time. Questions to ask about the character of any biography could include:

1. What does the character look like?
2. What does the character do?
3. Did the author include dialogue? What does the character say?
4. What does the character think about?
5. What do others say about this character?
6. Do you feel that the author's descriptions reflect the time in which the person lived and the issues of those times?
7. Does the character change during the course of his or her life?

Have students write descriptions of the biography character in order to understand the depth that biographers use to make these people come alive for the reader. For example, descriptions of Harriet Tubman might include the following:

She wanted to be free, more than stay alive.
She disguised herself.
She was clever.
She was 5 feet tall.
Her nickname was Moses.
She was determined, but sometimes afraid.
She was strong.
There were legends about her.
The Quakers helped her.
She wore a bandanna.
There was a wanted poster for her capture.
She was a big woman with a scar on her face.
Her two sisters were sold, and she never saw them again.
She knew the woods very well.
She traveled at night.

Another way to organize the character attributes is to cluster the descriptions into the different categories: actions, speech (including dialogue), thoughts, appearance, and what others say about this character

Actions:
When she reached Bucktown, it was daylight. She hoped that she wouldn't run into Dr. Thompson. But just in case, she invented a disguise. First, she bought two live chickens and tied them by their feet with

a cord. She tied the cord to her belt. Next, she pulled her wide sun bonnet down to hide her face and stooped over when she walked. Now she looked just like a little old woman taking her chickens to market. (p. 73)

Speech or dialogue:
"There's one of two things I've got a right to, liberty or death," Harriet explained years later. "If I could not have one, I would have the other. No man will take me back alive." (p. 37)

Appearance:
Wanted Poster—A drawing of a stocky black woman with a scar on her forehead wearing a bandanna appeared on the posters. Below the drawing a caption told that Harriet was about thirty-five years old. Her height was five feet. And it said that she could neither read nor write. (p. 69)

Others' comments:
One time Harriet was sitting at a train station when she overheard two men talking about her. They were trying to decide if she was the woman on the poster. Harriet had a book under her arm. Slowly she took it out and opened it. "No," she heard one of the men say at last. "She's reading. And the poster said the one they're after can't read." (p. 71)

Thoughts:
Harriet was grateful to the white woman. Yet she knew that escape would be especially dangerous for her. She might have one of her spells and be caught while sleeping on the road. With the big scar on her forehead, she would be easy to recognize. So, for the time being, Harriet kept the Quaker woman's word a secret in her heart. (p. 34)

After the students have collected descriptions of the person, design a Round Character Chart (see Figure 7.5) to illustrate how completely the author developed this character.

Figure 7.5   Round Character Chart

Actions	
Speech	
Appearance	
What Others Say	
Thoughts	

To determine if the author has accurately reflected the subject's times, the students will need to evaluate the character's actions, speech, and thoughts in relation to what was happening in the world at the time this person lived. Harriet Tubman's actions, speech, and thoughts revolved around freedom and the freedom of others.

A character that changes over time is a dynamic character, and in our read–aloud biography, Harriet changes over the years. As a young child she is shy, obedient, and afraid, but as she approaches adulthood, she becomes disciplined, courageous, independent, clever, and brave. When she was young, she did not understand people and why they behaved as they did, but as she became older, she developed a keen understanding of people.

Evaluating Authentic Settings

The settings in a biography support the character and must depict the times and the issues of the period. Because the settings are real places, the descriptions of the setting must be authentic. The following questions and chart will help students realize the importance of integral settings in biographies:

1. Does the author describe the settings in enough detail so that you can visualize this place or location?
2. Do the settings describe the times by including details? What are these details?
3. In the course of this person's life, did the settings change?

To answer the questions about setting, construct a Biography Settings Chart to help students visualize the settings (see Figure 7.6).

The Story of Harriet Tubman features a few settings. First of all, discuss the plantation in Dorchester County, Maryland, and compare the small one–room log hut in which Harriet lived to the Big House. The woods

Figure 7.6   Biography Settings Chart

Setting 1— The young child— Dorchester County— hut vs. Big House	Setting 2— The young adult— woods	Setting 3— Old age— home in Auburn, New York

is a second setting, and the class should discuss what she ate, where she hid, and how she felt while traveling through the woods. A third setting is Harriet's home in Auburn, New York.

Now have students give details about each setting. For example, items that would depict the times on the plantation might include: wagons, parlors, a ballroom, a cookhouse and horses for transportation. Finally, direct students to the Biography Settings Chart and discuss each setting in relation to the main character.

Understanding the Author's Style

When presenting a character in a biography, the author uses different techniques to depict the character. In this section, students will be introduced to flashbacks, dialogue, jackdaws, and anecdotes, and will gain a better understanding of how these techniques shape a character.

To fill in missing information, the author may use flashbacks, including anecdotes or dialogue. Here is an example of a flashback in the biography of Harriet Tubman:

> Terrified, Minty remembered how her two older sisters had been taken away, crying and screaming. They weren't much more than six or seven years old at the time. A slave trader from the South came to The Big House. Mr. Brodas sold Minty's sisters to him. The slave trader put chains around their ankles. Then he whipped them and forced them to begin walking South, chained together. Minty never saw her sisters again. (pp. 3–4)

Explain to students that an anecdote is a short account of a personal event. This is an anecdote that the author shared about Minty at the Cooks' home.

> Minty tried her best to do what Mrs. Cook wanted. But the yarn tangled in her fingers. Lint from the yarn rose in the air. It tickled Minty's nose and made her sneeze. Her eyes watered. But she wasn't allowed to stop. If she broke a piece of yarn, Mrs. Cook would lash her with a long, stinging whip. (p. 5)

A jackdaw is a collection of materials that represent an event in history or a specific time period. Jackdaws are used by authors to more fully develop the subject of their biography. Kate McMullan does not include any jackdaws in her biography about Harriett Tubman, however, other biographies do use photographs, newspaper clippings, and posters to help the reader understand the time and the subject of the biography. For example, Patricia McKissack and Fredrick McKissack include photographs, an insurance policy, an advertisement, and an inventory record in their biography *Sojourner Truth: Ain't I a Woman?* (1992). Carol Greene's picture biography *Laura Ingalls Wilder: Author of the Little House Books* (1990) includes authentic photographs of Wilder's home and family.

Realizing Theme

When all of the person's accomplishments are reviewed, students will realize that the theme is the *reason* why a biographical author writes about the life of a particular person. The theme of *Harriet Tubman: Conductor of the Underground Railroad* is freedom. This theme runs through the entire biography, first as Harriet achieves her own freedom and later as she devotes her life to freeing others as a conductor of the Underground Railroad.

Small-Group Guided Reading

Students should now be ready to experience biographies of their choosing. Before they begin reading, students can select the questions that they want to answer and the strategies that they will use to analyze the biography based on those shared during the read–aloud. Because they have worked through these questions and strategies with you, students should feel comfortable using them in small groups.

During this time, students also should devise additional questions they are interested in pursuing and fill in any charts that they think will help them understand their choice of a biography.

Questions for Small-Group Guided Reading

Ask students to answer these questions in their small guided–reading groups:

1. How did your group decide on which questions and activities to use? Were your questions and activities effective in helping to understand biographies?
2. How was this biography organized to show the life of the subject?

3. What were the major accomplishments of the person you read about?

4. How did the character change during his or her life?

5. How did the author write about the setting to make it authentic?

6. What special techniques did the author include to help you gain a deeper understanding of this character?

Independent Writing of Biographies

Students will better understand the elements of biographies when they write one themselves. The first step in writing a biography is to choose a subject. Share with students that biographies do not have to be written about only famous people, but can be written about ordinary people doing ordinary things. Picture books that you can share with students to illustrate this point include *My Great Aunt Arizona* (1992) by Gloria Houston or *Supergrandpa* (1991) by David Schwartz. These two books are appropriate for both age groups.

The next step in planning the biography is to collect information about the person who is the subject. One way to collect information about a living subject is to interview him or her and others who know this person, following Tompkins's (1998) three steps: planning the interview, conducting the interview, and presenting the results. Have students brainstorm questions that will allow the person being interviewed to tell their story in their own words. Remind students to remember how authors developed characters by collecting examples of their speech (including dialogue), their actions, their thoughts, and what others said. A list of what the person has accomplished should also be included. Remind students to collect anecdotes during the interview, as well as scenes to set as flashbacks. Once they have planned interview questions, students should organize the questions on note-cards, conduct the interview, and design a lifeline.

Curtis, a fifth-grade student, began his prewriting by thinking about things that he wanted to know about his great-grandmother and listing people who he could interview to find out more about her. For example, he listed two things that he wanted to know about: her school and parents. Then he decided that he wanted to interview his great grandpa, dad, and grandpa. Next, he planned his topics for the interview (see Figure 7.7 on page 146).

Figure 7.7   Topics for Curtis's Interviews

Year born?
Where she worked?
Where she lived?
Sisters or brothers—living or deceased?
Parents?
Foster children?
Children, grandchildren, great grandchildren?
Hobbies?
Married—when and where?
Funny stories?
College or school?

After the interview, the student may want to develop a lifeline for the subject, as Curtis did for his great–grandmother (Figure 7.8).

If students are taking notes on notecards, they can look through them to find the theme. What do all the facts, anecdotes, and dialogue say about the character? Why did the character accomplish what he or she did? What do you want to stress about this character?

Now students should be ready to write their biography using the techniques modeled and practiced in the read–aloud and applied in the guided reading activities. To begin their biographies, students may wish to experiment with using a catchy lead, which will hook the reader.

Curtis's published biography of his Great-Grandma Treresa begins on the next page.

Figure 7.8   Curtis's Great-Grandmother's Lifeline

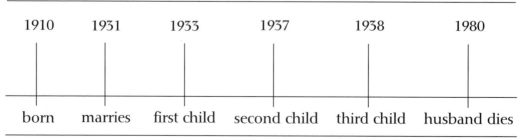

1910	1931	1933	1937	1938	1980
born	marries	first child	second child	third child	husband dies

Great-Grandma Treresa
by Curtis

It was a regular day. Treresa was getting ready for school. She over-heard her mother telling her three sisters to come join her in the kitchen so she could braid their hair. They didn't come downstairs, so her mother went up and heard the three sisters praying. After they had finished her mother declared it was the most beautiful prayer that she had ever heard and asked why they hadn't come to get their hair braided. They all had the same answer, they weren't going to school. They were too sick. Within the next month and a half, all three had died, each about two weeks apart. The family or doctors didn't know what sickness or disease they had died from. It was a very tragic loss for the whole family.

This story is about the life of my Great-Grandma Treresa. She had eleven brothers and sisters. She is third to the youngest. Her brothers are Martin, Adam, and August. Her sisters' names are Evelen, Barbara, Martha, Anne, Agnes, and Mary. Anne, Agnes, and Mary were the three children who died at childhood. She had two other siblings, but they died at birth. She also had two half brothers, John and Frank.

She attended a school called Green Meadow School. It had first to seventh grade only. It was a one room school with 52 kids and one teacher. She ran two and a half miles there and back. She didn't go to school in winter because of the cold and snow.

She liked to play games with her brothers, sisters, and neighbors. She had a 9 o'clock curfew. The children also liked listening to records on their victrola.

But she also had chores. Her parents made a deal with her and her brothers and sisters. For every dollar of milk they milked, they would get a nickel. That was a pretty good deal because you could get a sizable bag of candy for that much.

She worked at River Pines for two months. Then, she worked as a waitress in a Chicago restaurant. She got $7 if she worked during the day and $10 if she worked nights.

On Fourth of July weekend, she came to visit her mother who was ill. An uncle of hers had also come to visit, but since he had no car he asked a neighbor to give him a ride. Treresa's uncle's neighbor was named Henry Gagas. When Henry and Treresa's uncle got there, Henry saw pictures of Treresa on the piano. He immediately started asking questions. The first time Henry saw Treresa was when she was scrubbing the living room floor, which was wood. He asked her out on a date. She refused. He asked if he could treat her to a candy bar. She agreed.

They got married at Sacred Heart Church on July 7, 1931. After living with Henry's parents for five years, they moved into a woodshed they fixed into a house. They didn't have a honeymoon. Instead, they helped Henry's parents shock rye. After a couple of years, they built a farm. They continued farming for 45 years. Eventually, they passed the farm to their children.

They had five children. Don was their first child. He was born in a Chicago hospital in 1933. Their second child was Renetta. She was born in her home in 1937. Grace was their third child. She was born in their home in 1938. Henry Jr. was their fourth child. He was born in 1945. Diane was their last child, but after three months, she died from pneumonia. The other four children are still living and have children and grandchildren.

Her husband died in 1980. Her brother, Adam, and Treresa are the only children left from all 14 children of her family.

Questions for Writing a Biography

This assessment gives students the opportunity to reflect on the process of writing a biography following the activities in the Independent Writing of Biographies section. The questions ask students to provide a rationale for their choices of character, information gathering and organizing, theme identification, and the use of anecdotes, flashbacks, and jackdaws.

1. How did you select the character for your biography?
2. How did you collect the information about the person's life? Was this an effective way?
3. How did you decide to organize your information?
4. What special techniques, like anecdotes, flashbacks and jackdaws, did you include in your biography that helped others understand your character?
5. How would you describe the theme of your biography?
6. Would you like to share your biography with others?
7. Will you write another biography?

Biography Extensions

Ideas to extend the unit on biographies can be used to expand students' knowledge. During the small–group guided reading of biographies, give students the opportunity to design a Lifeline Poster. A Lifeline Poster is a poster that contains some significant artifacts that represent the person. Imposed on the illustration of this artifact is the person's lifeline. Examples of Lifeline Posters appear above and on page 150.

To bring closure to writing biographies, students could design covers for their biographies by illustrating significant parts of their subjects' lives. The cover Curtis made for his published biography appears on page 151.

Another way to extend this unit is to share books by authors who write from a different point of view. For example, Lawson's biographies are written from the point of view of a horse in *Mr. Revere and I* and a mouse in *Ben and Me*. F.N. Monjo wrote biographies from a child's point of view in *Grand Papa and Ellen Aroon: Being the Account of Some of the Happy*

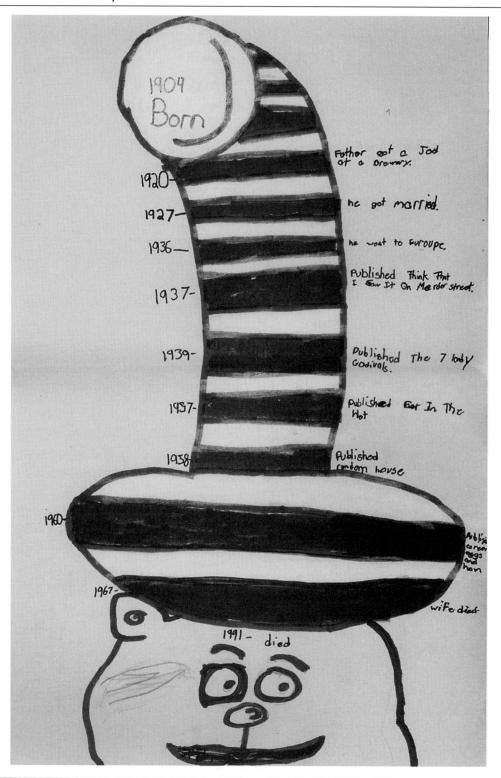

Times Spent Together by Thomas Jefferson and His Favorite Granddaughter and *Me and Willie and Pa: The Story of Abraham Lincoln and His Son Tad.*

To show students the importance of accuracy in biographies, compare how different authors portray the same person. For example, the biography of Harriet Tubman written by Kate McMullan could be compared with other biographies of Harriet Tubman: Ann McGovern's biography *Wanted Dead or Alive: The True Story of Harriet Tubman* (1965) or David Adler's *A Picture Book of Harriet Tubman* (1992). Ask students about any inconsistencies. Zarnowski (1998) suggests that "even readers in the primary grades can begin to deal with contradictory versions of historical events" (p. 350). She cites two biographies that give different accounts of Louis Armstrong's youth: *Satchmo's Blues* (1996) by Alan Schroeder and *If I Only Had a Horn: Young Louis Armstrong* (1997) by Roxanne Orgill. Which version do the students believe? Why? How could two authors come up with different information?

Curtis's cover sheet

Designing jackdaws should not be limited to the past. For example, if a student writes a biography about a contemporary person, he or she should be encouraged to collect pictures or artifacts that represent this person. The read–aloud book could be extended by collecting jackdaws that represent the time and the character of the biography. Examples of jackdaws that might have been added to the biography *Harriet Tubman: Conductor of the Underground Railroad* include newspaper clippings from the time that Harriet was a conductor of the Underground Railroad; a map of where Harriet was born in Maryland; a map showing where she traveled on the Underground Railroad; copies of songs, recipes, or artwork from the time period; and a copy of the Fugitive Slave Law and the Thirteenth Amendment to the Constitution.

The study of biographies leads nicely into the study of autobiographies, a subgenre of biographies. The same questions and activities that were used for biographies can be used for autobiographies. A bibliography of biographies and autobiographies is included at the end of this book on page 170.

Summary

The study of biographies is really an exercise in character development. Biography authors take the reader into the character's life by starting the story in an interesting way that hooks the reader into wanting to read more. Readers follow this character's life and accomplishments as the author develops a dynamic, round character by including flashbacks, anecdotes, and jackdaws. The in–depth study of the character leads the reader to discover the theme or why the author wrote this biography.

References

Calkins, L. (1986). *The art of teaching writing*. Portsmouth, NH: Heinemann.

Calkins, L.M. (1994). *The art of teaching writing*. Portsmouth, NH: Heinemann.

Cavelti, J. (1976). *Adventure, mystery, and romance*. Chicago: University of Chicago Press.

Corcoran, B. (1992). Reader stance: From willed aesthetic to discursive construction. In J. Many & C. Cox (Eds.), *Reader stance and literary understanding*. Norwood, NJ: Ablex.

Cornett, C. (1999). *Integrating literature and the arts throughout the curriculum*. Upper Saddle River, NJ: Simon & Schuster.

Cullinan, B., & Galda, L. (1994). *Literature and the child*. Orlando, FL: Harcourt College Publishers.

Glazer, J. (1997). *Literature for young children*. Upper Saddle River, NJ: Merrill/Prentice Hall.

Graves, D. (1983). *Writing teachers and children at work*. Portsmouth, NH: Heinemann.

Harste, J., Short, K., & Burke, C. (1988). *Creating classrooms for authors*. Portsmouth, NH: Heinemann.

Hickman, J., & Cullinan, B. (Eds.). (1989). *Children's literature in the classroom*. Needham Heights, MA: Christopher–Gordon.

Hillman, J. (1999). *Discovering children's literature*. Upper Saddle River, NJ: Prentice Hall.

Howe, J. (1990). Writing mysteries for children. *Horn Book Magazine, LXVI*, 2, 178–183.

Huck, C., Helper, S., Hickman., J., & Kiefer, B. (1997). *Children's literature in the elementary school*. Boston: McGraw–Hill.

Jacobs, J., & Tunnel, M.O. (1996). *Children's literature briefly*. Englewood Cliffs, NJ: Prentice–Hall.

Johnson, C. (Ed.). (1985). *Myths, legends, and folk tales from the Hmong of Laos*. St. Paul, MN: Linguistics Department, MacCalaster College.

Johnson, T.D., & Louis, D.R. (1987). *Literacy through literature*. Portsmouth, NH: Heinemann.

Livo, N.J., & Cha, D. (1991). *Folk Stories of the Hmong*. Englewood, CO: Libraries Unlimited.

Lukens, R.J. (1999). *Critical handbook of children's literature*. New York: Addison–Wesley.

Macon, J.M., Bewell, D., & Vogt, M.E. (1991). *Responses to literature: Grades K–8*. Newark, DE: International Reading Association.

Madsen, L. (1976). *Fantasy in children's literature: A generic study*. Masters thesis, Utah State University, Logan.

Neeld, E.C. (1986). *Writing*. Glenview, IL: Scott Foresman.

Norton, D. (1995). *Through the eyes of a child*. Englewood Cliffs, NJ: Prentice Hall.

Rosenblatt, L.M. (1978). *The reader, the text, the poem*. Carbondale, IL: Southern Illinois University Press.

Routman, R. (1991). *Invitations*. Portsmouth, NH: Heinemann.

Russell, D.L. (1997). *Literature for children*. New York: Longman.

Smith, F. (1983). Reading like a writer. *Language Arts, 60*, 558–567.

Sutherland, Z. (1997). *Children & books*. New York: Longman.

Tomlison, C.M., & Lynch–Brown, C. (1996). *Essentials of children's literature*. Boston: Allyn & Bacon.

Tompkins, G.E., & McGee, L.M. (1993). *Teaching reading with literature*. New York: Macmillan.

Tompkins, G.E. (1994). *Teaching writing: Balancing process and product*. New York: Merrill.

Tompkins, G.E. (1998). *Language arts content and teaching strategies*. Upper Saddle River, NJ: Merrill.

Thompson, S. (1955–1958). *Motif index of folk literature*. Bloomington, IN: Indiana University Press.

Tonjes, M., Wolpow, R., & Zintz, M.V. (1999). *Integrated content literacy*. Boston: McGraw–Hill.

Zarnowski, M. (1998). Coming out from under the spell of stories: Critiquing historical narratives. *The New Advocate, 11*, 345–356.

Zarrillo, J., & Cox, C. (1992). Efferent and aesthetic teaching. In J. Many & C. Cox (Eds.), *Reader stance and literary understanding*. Norwood, NJ: Ablex.

Children's Literature References

Realistic Fiction

Family and Friends Stories

Ackerman, K. (1993). *The leaves in october*. New York: Simon & Schuster Children's.

Armstrong, R. (1997). *Drew and the homeboy question*. New York: HarperCollins.

Bauer, M.D. (1986). *On my honor*. Boston: Houghton Mifflin.

Blume, J. (1982). *Tiger Eyes*. New York: Bantam Doubleday.

Bunting, E. (1994). *Sharing Susan*. New York: HarperCollins Children's Books.

Byars, B. (1987). *The Pinballs*. New York: HarperCollins Children's Books.

Caseley, J. (1997). *Dorothy's darkest days*. New York: Greenwillow.

Cleary, B. (1979). *Ramona and her mother*. New York: Avon.

Cleary, B. (1990). *Beezus and Ramona*. New York: Avon.

Cleary, B. (1990). *Henry and Beezus*. New York: Avon.

Cleary, B. (1990). *Henry and Ribsy*. New York: Avon.

Cleary, B. (1990). *Henry and the paper route*. New York: Avon.

Cleary, B. (1990). *Muggie Maggie*. New York: Avon.

Cleary, B. (1990). *Ramona and her father*. New York: Avon.

Cleary, B. (1992). *Ramona Quimby, age eight*. New York: Avon.

Cleary, B. (1992). *Ramona the pest*. New York: Avon.

Cleary, B. (1995). *Ramona forever*. New York: Avon.

Cleary, B. (1995). *Ramona the brave*. New York: Avon.

Cleary, B. (1996). *Dear Mr. Henshaw*. New York: Avon.

Cleary, B. (1996). *Henry Huggins*. New York: Avon.

Cooney, C. (1993). *Whatever happened to Janie?* New York: Delacorte.

Cooney, C. (1996). *The face on the milk carton*. New York: Bantam Doubleday Dell.

Cormier, R. (1986). *The chocolate war*. New York: Dell.

Crew, L. (1992). *Someday I'll laugh*. New York: Delacourt.

Curtis, C.P. (1995). *The Watsons go to Birmingham—1963*. New York: Bantam Doubleday Dell.

DeClements, B. (1995). *Sixth grade can really kill you*. New York: Scholastic.

Duffey, B. (1993). *How to be cool in the third grade*. New York: Puffin.

Fenner, C. (1995). *Yolonda's genius*. New York: Aladdin Paperbacks.

Fletcher, R. (1996). *Fig pudding*. New York: Bantam Doubleday Dell.

Fletcher, R. (1997). *Spider boy*. New York: Clarion.

Fox, P. (1997). *Radiance descending*. New York: DK INK.

Gilson, J. (1991). *Hello, my name is Scrambled Eggs*. New York: Lothrop, Lee & Shepard.

Hoffman, M. (1991). *Amazing Grace*. New York: Dial Books for Young Readers.

Hurwitz, J. (1989). *Aldo ice cream*. New York: Penguin.

Konigsburg, E.L. (1970). *From the mixed-up files of Mrs. Basil E. Frankweiler*. New York: Bantam Doubleday Dell.

Konigsburg, E.L. (1996). *The view from Saturday*. New York: Atheneum.

Kroll, V. (1997). *Butterfly boy*. Honesdale, PA: Boyds Mills.

Lowry, L. (1977). *A summer to die*. Boston: Houghton Mifflin.

McKay, L. (1998). *Journey home*. New York: Lee & Low.

Mills, C. (1997). *Losers, Inc.* New York: Farrar, Straus & Giroux.

Myers, W.D. (1992). *Somewhere in the darkness*. New York: Scholastic.

Naidoo, B. (1986). *Journey to Jo'burg: A South African story*. New York: HarperCollins Children's Books.

Park, B. (1995). *Mick Harte was here*. New York: Apple Soup.

Patterson, K. (1977). *Bridge to Terabithia*. New York: HarperCollins Children's Books.

Patterson, K. (1978). *The great Gilly Hopkins*. New York: Puffin.

Patterson, K. (1989). *Park's quest*. New York: Puffin.

Patterson, K. (1996). *Flip-flop girl*. New York: Dutton Children's Books.

Rodowsky, C. (1998). *The turnabout shop*. New York: Farrar, Straus & Giroux.

Sachs, M. (1996). *The bears' house*. New York: Puffin.

Smith, R.K. (1984). *War with grandpa*. New York: Dell.

Snyder, Z.K. (1995). *The diamond war*. New York: Bantam Doubleday Dell.

Spinelli, J. (1990). *Maniac Magee*. Boston: Little, Brown.

Taylor, M.D. (1976). *Roll of thunder, hear my cry*. New York: Puffin.

Twain, M. (1987). *The adventures of Tom Sawyer*. New York: Viking.

Voigt, C. (1982). *Dicey's song*. New York: Fawcett.

Animal Stories

Blake, R.J. (1997). *Akiak: A tale from the Iditarod*. New York: Philomel.

Burnford, S. (1996). *The incredible journey*. New York: Laureleaf.

Cleary, B. (1964). *Ribsy*. New York: Avon.

Cleary, B. (1991). *Strider*. New York: Avon.

Gardiner, J.R. (1980). *Stone fox*. New York: HarperCollins Children's Books.

Henry, M. (1990). *Misty of Chincoteague*. New York: Simon & Schuster Children's.

Lapp, E. (1988). *Orphaned pup*. New York: Scholastic.

Naylor, P.R. (1991). *Shiloh*. New York: Simon & Schuster Children's.

Naylor, P.R. (1996). *Shiloh season*. New York: Simon & Schuster Children's.

Naylor, P.R. (1997). *Saving Shiloh*. New York: Simon & Schuster Children's.

Rawls, W. (1996). *Where the red fern grows*. New York: Bantam Doubleday Dell.

Taylor, T. (1983). *The trouble with Tuck*. New York: Avon.

Humorous

Blume, J. (1972). *Tales of a fourth grade nothing*. New York: Dutton Children's Books.

Blume, J. (1981). *Superfudge*. New York: Dutton Children's Books.

Blume, J. (1990). *Fudge-a-mania*. New York: Dutton Children's Books.

Hurwitz, J. (1987). *Class clown*. New York: Scholastic.

Lowry, L. (1979). *Anastasia Krupnik*. Boston: Houghton Mifflin.

Lowry, L. (1990). *All about Sam*. Boston: Houghton Mifflin.

Lowry, L. (1992). *Attaboy, Sam!* Boston: Houghton Mifflin.

Park, B. (1982). *Skinnybones*. New York: Random House.

Sachar, L. (1985). *Sideways stories from Wayside School*. New York: Avon.

Sachar, L. (1987). *There's a boy in the girls' bathroom*. New York: Bullseye Books.

Sachar, L. (1990). *Wayside School is falling down*. New York: Avon.

Sachar, L. (1991). *Dogs don't tell jokes*. New York: Random House.

Spinelli, J. (1993). *Fourth grade rats*. New York: Scholastic.

Spinelli, J. (1996). *Crash*. New York: Alfred A. Knopf.

Survival

Cole, B. (1987). *The goats*. New York: Bantam Doubleday Dell.

George, J.C. (1972). *Julie of the wolves*. Scranton, PA: HarperCollins Children's Books.

George, J.C. (1988). *My side of the mountain*. New York: Dutton Children's Books.

George, J.C. (1990). *On the far side of the mountain*. New York: Dutton Children's Books.

George, J.C. (1997). *Julie's wolf pack*. Scranton: HarperCollins Children's Books.

Hill, K. (1990). *Toughboy & sister*. New York: The Trumpet Club.

Holcomb, J.K. (1998). *The chinquapin tree*. New York: Marshall Cavendish.

Paulsen, G. (1985). *Dogsong*. New York: Puffin.

Paulsen, G. (1987). *Hatchet*. New York: Simon & Schuster Children's.

Paulsen, G. (1990). *Canyons*. New York: Bantam Doubleday Dell.
Paulsen, G. (1991). *The river*. New York: Bantam Doubleday Dell.
Taylor, T. (1977). *The cay*. New York: Bantam Doubleday Dell.
Taylor, T. (1993). *Timothy of the cay*. New York: Bantam Doubleday Dell.

Sports

Bledsoe, L. (1995). *The big bike race*. New York: Avon.
Bughes, D. (1995). *Back-up star*. New York: Bullseye.
Christopher, M. (1985). *The fox steals home*. Boston: Little, Brown.
Christopher, M. (1990). *Baseball pals*. Boston: Little, Brown.
Christopher, M. (1991). *Skateboard tough*. Boston: Little, Brown.
Christopher, M. (1997). *Snowboard maverick*. Boston: Little, Brown.
Christopher, M. (1998). *Spike it!* Boston: Little, Brown.
Christopher, M. (1999). *Snowboard showdown*. Boston: Little, Brown.
Herman, H. (1994). *Super hoops: Crashing the boards*. New York: Bantam.
Herman, H. (1996). *Monster jam*. New York: Banton Books.
Hiser, C. (1991). *Dog on third base*. New York: Minstrel Books.
Myers, W.D. (1992). *Me, Mop, and the Moondance Kid*. New York: Doubleday.
Myers, W.D. (1992). *Mop, Moondance and the Nagasaki Knights*. New York: Yearling Books.
O'Dell, S. (1988). *Black star, bright dawn*. New York: Fawcett.
Slote, A. (1990). *The trading game*. New York: HarperCollins Children's Books.
Weaver, R. (1968). *Nice guy, go home*. New York: HarperCollins.

Juvenile Mysteries

Bunting, E. (1990). *Is anybody there?* New York: Harper Trophy.
Bunting, E. (1992). *Coffin on a case!* New York: Harper Trophy.
Byars, B. (1993). *Wanted...Mud Blossom*. New York: Yearling Books.
Carter, P. (1987). *Bury the dead*. New York: Farrar, Straus & Giroux.
Cavanagh, H. (1996). *The last piper*. New York: Simon & Schuster Children's.
Clifford, E. (1994). *Harvey's mystifying raccoon mix-up*. Boston: Houghton Mifflin.
Conrad, P. (1991). *Stonewords: A ghost story*. New York: HarperCollins Juvenile Books.
Duncan, L. (1988). *The twisted window*. Boston: Laurel Leaf.
Duncan, L. (1991). *The third eye*. Boston: Laurel Leaf.
Duncan, L. (1994). *Who killed my daughter?* New York: Dell.
Duncan, L. (1997). *Down a dark hall*. Boston: Laurel Leaf.

Fleischman, S. (1991). *The midnight horse*. New York: Greenwillow.

Fleischman, S. (1997). *The 13th floor*. New York: Yearling Books.

George, J.C. (1992). *Who really killed cock robin? An ecological mystery*. New York: HarperCollins Children's Books.

Griffin, P.R. (1992). *The treasure bird*. New York: Simon & Schuster Children's.

Haddix, M.P. (1995). *Running out of time*. New York: Simon & Schuster Children's.

Hahn, M.D. (1989). *Following the mystery man*. New York: Simon & Schuster Children's.

Hahn, M.D. (1991). *The dead man in Indian Creek*. New York: Avon.

Hall, L. (1988). *Ride a dark horse*. New York: Avon.

Hall, L. (1990). *The tormentors*. Orlando, FL: Harcourt Brace.

Hamilton, V. (1968). *The house of Dies Drear*. New York: Macmillan.

Herzig, A.C., & Maki, J.L. (1993). *Mystery on October Road*. New York: Scholastic.

Hildick, E.W. (1995). *Hester Bidgood: Investigatrix of evil deeds*. New York: Simon & Schuster Children's.

Hildick, E.W. (1996). *The case of the wiggling wig: Curious clues lead to a devious crime in the 25th McGurk mystery*. New York: Simon & Schuster Children's.

Lasky, K. (1991). *Double trouble squared: A Starbuck family adventure*. San Diego: Harcourt Brace.

Lasky, K. (1998). *Alice, Rose, and Sam*. New York: Hyperion.

Lawrence, I. (1998). *The wreckers*. New York: Delacorte.

Lexau, J.M. (1994). *Trouble will find you*. Boston: Houghton Mifflin.

Macaulay, D. (1979). *The motel of the mysteries*. Boston: Houghton Miffllin.

Mariconda, B. (1998). *Turn the cup around*. New York: Bantom Doubleday Dell.

McGraw, E. (1993). *Tangled webb*. New York: Simon & Schuster Children's.

Miller, D. (1996). *The clearing*. Old Tappan, NJ: Atheneum.

Miller, M. (1996). *Scene of the crime: Death comes to dinner*. New York: Scholastic.

Naylor, P.R. (1993). *The face in the Bessledorf Funeral Parlor*. New York: Simon & Schuster Children's.

Neufeld, J. (1996). *Gaps in stone walls*. Old Tappan, NJ: Atheneum.

Page, K.H. (1998). *Christie & Company down east*. New York: Simon & Schuster Children's Books.

Pryor, B. (1995). *Marvelous Marvin and the pioneer ghost*. New York: Morrow.

Raskin, E. (1992). *The westing game*. New York: Puffin.

Roberts, W.D. (1990). *Megan's island*. New York: Simon & Schuster Children's.

Roberts, W.D. (1990). *To grandmother's house we go.* New York: Simon & Schuster Children's.

Roberts, W.D. (1994). *The absolutely true story...How I visited Yellowstone Park with the terrible Rupes.* New York: Simon & Schuster Children's.

Roberts, W.D. (1994). *Caught.* New York: Simon & Schuster Children's.

Roberts, W.D. (1998). *The kidnappers.* Old Tappan, NJ: Atheneum.

Roberts, W.D. (1998). *Secrets at Hidden Valley.* New York: Simon & Schuster Children's Books.

Sachar, Louis. (1998). *Holes.* New York: Farrar, Straus & Giroux.

Schwandt, S. (1995). *The last goodie.* Minneapolis, MN: FreeSpirit Publishing.

Skurzynski, G., & Ferguson, A. (1997). *Wolf stalker.* Washington, DC: National Geographic Society.

Slote, A. (1991). *Finding Buck McHenry.* New York: HarperCollins Children's Books.

Springer, N. (1994). *Toughing it.* Orlando, FL: Harcourt Brace.

Springer, N. (1998). *Looking for Jamie Bridger.* New York: Dial Books for Young Readers.

Steiner, B.A. (1990). *Ghost cave.* Orlando, FL: Harcourt Brace.

Stevenson, J. (1995). *The bones in the cliff.* New York: Greenwillow Books.

Van Allsburg, C. (1992). *The widow's broom.* Boston: Houghton Mifflin.

Van Draanen, W. (1998). *Sammy Keyes and the hotel thief.* New York: Alfred A. Knopf Books for Young Readers.

Wallace, B.B. (1993). *Peppermints in the parlor.* New York: Macmillan Children's Book Group.

Wallace, B.B. (1993). *The twin in the tavern.* New York: Simon & Schuster Children's.

Wallace, B.B. (1997). *Sparrows in the scullery.* New York: Simon & Schuster Children's.

Wortis, A. (1988). *Something upstairs.* New York: Orchard Books.

Wulffson, D. (1994). *Six minute mysteries.* Los Angeles: Lowell House Juvenile.

Wulffson, D. (1995). *More six minute mysteries.* Los Angeles: Lowell House Juvenile.

Folktales

Wonder Tales

Adams, E.B. (1984). *Korean Cinderella.* Ill. D.H. Choi. Seoul, Korea: Seoul International Tourist Publishing Company.

Asbjorsen, P.C., & Moe, J. (1953). *East o' the sun and west o' the moon*. New York: Macmillan.

Beckett, S. (1974). *Hansel and Gretel*. Ill. S. Beckett. New York: Random House.

Carrick, C. (1989). *Aladdin and the wonderful lamp*. New York: Scholastic.

Cauley, L.B. (1983). *Jack and the beanstalk*. New York: Putnam.

Climo, S. (1989). *The Egyptian Cinderella*. Ill. R. Heller. New York: Crowell.

Coady, C. (1991). *Little Red Riding Hood*. New York: Dutton Children's Books.

Coburn, J.R. (1996). *Jovanah: A Hmong Cinderella*. Arcadia, CA: Shen's Books.

Compton, J. (1994). *Ashpet*. New York: Holiday House.

Cushing, F.H. (1972). The poor turkey girl. In M.A. Nelson, *A comparative anthology of children's literature*. New York: Holt, Rinehart & Winston.

Delamar, D. (1993). *Cinderella*. New York: Green Tiger Press.

DePaola, T. (1975). *Strega Nona: An old tale retold*. San Diego: Harcourt.

Gag, W. (Illustrator). (1999). *Snow White and the seven dwarfs*.

Goodall, J.S. (1988). *Little Red Riding Hood*. New York: MacMillan.

Greaves, M. (1992). *Tattercoats*. New York: Crown Books for Young Readers.

Green, R.L. (1972). The girl with the red rose slipper. In M.A. Nelson, *A comparative anthology of children's literature*. New York: Holt, Rinehart & Winston.

Grimm, J., & Grimm, W. (1986). *Little red riding hood*. New York: Scholastic.

Grimm, J., & Grimm, W. (1987). *Snow White and the seven dwarfs* (R. Jarrell, Trans.). New York: Farrar, Straus & Giroux.

Grimm, J., & Grimm, W. (1988). *Hansel and Gretel* (E.D. Crawford, Trans.). New York: Scholastic.

Grimm, J., & Grimm, W. (1991). *The seven ravens*. New York: Simon & Schuster Children's.

Grimm, J., & Grimm, W. (1994). *Sleeping beauty*. Ill. D. Schulz. St. Petersburg: Worthington Press.

Harper, W. (1967). *The Gunniwolf*. Ill. W. Wiesner. New York: Trumpet Book Club.

Hayes, S. (Ed.). (1997). *The Candlewick book of fairy tales*. Ill. P.J. Lynch. Cambridge, MA: Candlewick Press.

Heins, P. (1974). *Snow White*. Boston: Little, Brown.

Hickox, R. (1998). *The golden sandal: A Middle Eastern Cinderella*. New York: Holiday House.

Hooks, W.H. (1987). *Moss gown*. Ill. D. Carrick. New York: Clarion Books.

Huck, C. (1994). *Princess furball.* Ill. by A. Lobel. New York: Greenwillow.

Hunt, L.C. (1972). A Chinese Cinderella. In M.A. Nelson, *A comparative anthology of children's literature.* New York: Holt, Rinehart & Winston.

Hyman, T.S. (1983). *Little red riding hood.* Ill. T. Schart. New York: Holiday House.

Jarrell, F. (1980). *Snow White and the seven dwarfs.* New York: Scholastic.

Kimmel, E.A. (1991). *Baba Yaga: A Russian folktale.* Ill. M. Lloyd. New York: Holiday House.

Lesser, R. (1999). *Hansel and Gretel.* Ill. P.O. Zeblinsky. New York: Dutton.

Lewis, P. (1994). *The frog princess.* New York: Dial Books for Young Readers.

Littledale, F. (1980). *Snow White and the seven dwarfs.* New York: Scholastic.

Louie, A. (1982). *Yeh-Shen: A Cinderella story from China.* Ill. E. Young. New York: Philomel.

MacMillan, C. (1992). The Indian Cinderella. In J. Trealease, *Hey! listen to this: Stories to read aloud.* New York: Penguin.

Mahy, M. (1990). *The seven Chinese brothers.* New York: Scholastic.

Martin, R. (1992). *The rough-face girl.* New York: Putnam.

Mikolaycak, C. (1984). *Babushka: An old Russian folktale.* New York: Holiday House.

Nelson, M. (1972). The girl with the red rose slipper. In A. Nelson, *A comparative anthology of children's literature.* New York: Holt, Rinehart & Winston.

Perrault, C. (1949). *The sleeping beauty in the wood* (P.H. Muir, Trans.). Ill. S. Savage. New York: The Limited Editions Club.

Perrault, C. (1985). *Cinderella.* Ill. S. Jeffers. New York: Dial Books for Young Readers.

Perrault, C. (1985). *Cinderella.* Retold by Amy Ehlich. New York: Dial Books for Young Readers.

Perrault, C. (1991). *Sleeping beauty and other classic fairy tales.* New York: Random House.

Rhee, N. (1993). *Magic spring: A Korean folktale.* New York: Putnam.

Ross, T. (1990). *Stone soup.* New York: Dial Books for Young Readers.

Sanderson, R. (1990). *The twelve dancing princesses.* Boston: Little, Brown.

Steele, F.A. (1976). *Tattercoats.* Ill. D. Goode. New York: Bradbury Press.

Steptoe, J. (1987). *Mufaro's beautiful daughters: An African tale.* Ill. C. Kohen. New York: Lothrop, Lee & Shepard.

Steptoe, J. (1987). *Sootface: An Ojibwa Cinderella story.* New York: Bantam Doubleday Dell.

Steptoe, J. (1989). *The talking eggs.* New York: Dial Books for Young Readers.

Tan, A. (1992). *The moon lady*. Ill. G. Schields. New York: Macmillan.

Trout, L. (1975). Cinderella: A tale of the Zuni Indians. In *Tales, folk, and tomfoolery: A collection of folklore*. New York: Scholastic.

Vuong, L.D. (1991). *The brocaded slipper and other Vietnamese tales*. New York: HarperCollins.

Wang, R.C. (1991). *The fourth question: A Chinese tale*. New York: Holiday House.

Wilson, B.K. (1993). *Wishbones: A folktale of China*. Ill. M. So. New York: Macmillan.

Winthrop, E. (1991). *Vasilissa the Beautiful: A Russian folktale*. New York: HarperCollins.

Yagawa, S. (1981). *The Crane Wife*. Retold by Suekichi Akaba. New York: Morrow.

Yep, L. (1993). *The shell woman and the king: A Chinese folktale*. Ill. Y. Ming-Yi. New York: Dial Books for Young Readers.

Yolen, J. (1986). *The sleeping beauty*. Ill. R. Sanderson. New York: Ariel Books/Alfred A. Knopf.

Yoshiko, U. (1994). *The wise old woman*. New York: Margaret K. McElderry Books.

Young, E. (1989). *Lon Po Po: A red riding hood story from China*. New York: Putnam.

Beast Tales

Asbjorsen, P.C., & Moe, J. (1957). *The three billy goats gruff*. Retold by Marcia Brown. New York: Harcourt.

Brett, J. (1987). *Goldilocks and the three bears*. New York: Putnam.

Cauley, L.B. (1981). *Goldilocks and the three bears*. New York: Putnam.

Galdone, P. (1972). *The three bears*. New York: Seabury.

Galdone, P. (1979). *The little red hen*. New York: Clarion.

Galdone, P. (1979). *The three billy goats gruff*. New York: Clarion.

Galdone, P. (1981). *The three little pigs*. New York: Clarion.

Galdone, P. (1984). *The gingerbread boy*. New York: Clarion.

Jacobs, J. (1980). *The story of the three little pigs*. New York: Putnam.

Rounds, G. (1993). *The three billy goats gruff*. New York: Holiday House.

Cumulative Tales

Aardema, V. (1981). *Bringing the rain to Kapiti Plain*. New York: Dial Books for Young Readers.

Aardema, V. (1994). Goso the teacher. In V. Aardema (Ed.), *Misoso: Once upon a time tales from Africa*. New York: Knopf.

Aardema, V. (1994). No, Boconono! In V. Aardema (Ed.), *Misoso: Once upon a time tales from Africa*. New York: Knopf.

Asbjorsen, P., & Moe, J. (1998). *The pancake boy: An old Norwegian folk tale*. Retold by Lorinda Bryan Cauley. New York: Putnam.

Appiah, P. (1989). The Gift of Densu. In *Tales of an Ashanti father*. Boston: Beacon Press.

Brett, J. (1989). *The mitten*. New York: Putnam.

Brown, M. (1972). *The bun: A tale from Russia*. San Diego, CA: Harcourt Brace.

Butler, S. (1991). *Henny Penny*. New York: Tambourine.

Galdone, P. (1961). *The house that Jack built*. New York: McGraw–Hill.

Galdone, P. (1984). *The gingerbread boy*. New York: Clarion.

Galdone, P. (1985). *Cat goes fiddle-i-fee*. New York: Clarion.

Kent, R. (1953). *The fat cat: A Danish folktale*. New York: Scholastic.

Sawyer, R. (1978). *Journey cake, ho!* New York: Viking.

Stevens, J. (1985). *The house that Jack built*. New York: Holiday House.

Wood, A. (1984). *The napping house*. San Diego: Harcourt Brace.

Pourquoi Stories

Aardema, V. (1975). *Why mosquitoes buzz in people's ears*. New York: Dial.

Aardema, V. (1994). Half–A–Ball–Of–Keni. *In Misoso: Once upon a time tales from Africa*. New York: Scholastic.

Appiah, P. (1976). Why the leopard has spots. In *Tales of an Ashanti Father*. Boston: Beacon Press.

Appiah, P. (1976). Why the lion roars. In *Tales of an Ashanti father*. Boston: Beacon Press.

Appiah, P. (1976). Why the lizard stretches his neck. In *Tales of an Ashanti father*. Boston: Beacon Press.

Appiah, P. (1976). Why the snake has no legs. In *Tales of an Ashanti father*. Boston: Beacon Press.

Begay, S. (1976). Why bears have short tails. In B. Baylor (Ed.), *And it is still that way*. Sante Fe, NM: Trails West Publishing.

Bowden, J.C. (1979). *Why the tides ebb and flow*. Boston: Houghton Mifflin.

Bruchac, J. (1992). How butterflies came to be. In *Native American animal stories*. Golden, CO: Fulcrum.

Bruchac, J. (1992). How the fawn got its spots. In *Native American animal stories*. Golden, CO: Fulcrum.

Bruchac, J. (1992). How the people hunted the moose. In *Native American animal stories*. Golden, CO: Fulcrum.

Bruchac, J. (1992). Why coyote has yellow eyes. In *Native American animal stories*. Golden, CO: Fulcrum.

Bruchac, J. (1992). Why possum has a naked tail. In *Native American animal stories*. Golden, CO: Fulcrum.

Dayrell, E. (1990). *Why the sun and the moon live in the sky: An African folktale*. New York: Scholastic.

Dove, M. (1990). Why badger is so humble. In *Coyote stories*. Lincoln, NE: University of Nebraska Press.

Dove, M. (1990). Why gartersnake wears a green blanket. In *Coyote stories*. Lincoln, NE: University of Nebraska Press.

Dove, M. (1990). Why mosquitoes bite people. In *Coyote stories*. Lincoln, NE: University of Nebraska Press.

Dove, M. (1990). Why spider has such long legs. In *Coyote stories*. Lincoln, NE: University of Nebraska Press.

Dove, M. (1990). Why skunk's tail is black and white. In *Coyote stories*. Lincoln, NE: University of Nebraska Press.

French, V. (1993). *Why the sea is salt*. Cambridge, MA: Candlewick Press.

Gerson, M. (1992). *Why the sky is far away*. New York: Little, Brown.

Gerson, M. (1994). *How night came from the sea: A story from Brazil*. New York: Little, Brown.

Giff, C. (1976). Why rattlesnake has fangs. In B. Baylor (Ed.), *And it is still that way*. Santa Fe, NM: Trails West Publishing.

Johnson, C. (Ed.). (1985). Why farmers have to carry their crops. In *Myths, Legends, and Folktales from the Hmong*. St. Paul, MN: Macalaster College.

Jones, G. (1992). Why the bear has a stumpy tail. In *Scandinavian legends and folk-tales*. Oxford, England: Oxford University Press.

Joseph, D. (1976). Why birds live in our villages. In B. Baylor (Ed.), *And it is still that way*. Santa Fe, NM: Trails West Publishing.

Kab, P.R., & Kev, Y.R. (1990). Why are there stars in the sky? In L. Vang & J. Lewis (Eds.), *Grandmother's path: grandfather's way*. Rancho Corova, CA: Authors.

Kab, P.R., & Kev, Y.R. (1990). Why we have day and night. In L. Vang & J. Lewis (Eds.), *Grandmother's path: grandfather's way*. Rancho Corova, CA: Authors.

Livo, N., & Cha, D. (Eds.). (1991). Why the Hmong live on mountains. In *Folk Stories of the Hmong*. Englewood, CO: Libraries Unlimited.

Orosco, D. (1976). How oceans came to be. In B. Baylor (Ed.), *And it is still that way*. Santa Fe, NM: Trails West Publishing.

Oughton, J. (1992). *How the stars fell into the sky*. Boston: Houghton Mifflin.

Skacy, M. (1976). Why dogs sniff. In B. Baylor (Ed.), *And it is still that way*. Santa Fe, NM: Trails West Publishing.

Fables

Bierhorst, J. (1987). *Doctor Coyote: A Native American Aesop's fable*. New York: Macmillan.

Brett, J. (1994). *Town mouse, country mouse*. New York: Macmillan.

Brown, M. (1961). *Once a mouse*. New York: Scribner's.

Cauley, L.B. (1984). *The town mouse and the country mouse*. New York: Putnam.

Demi. (1996). *The dragon's tale and other animal fables of the Chinese zodiac*. New York: Henry Holt & Company.

Hague, M. (1999). *Aesop's fables*. New York: Henry Holt & Company.

Lobel, A. (1980). *Fables*. New York: HarperCollins.

Yolen, J. (1995). *A sip of Aesop*. New York: Scholastic.

Young, E. (1992). *Seven blind mice*. New York: Philomel.

Winter, M. (1994). *The Aesop for children*. New York: Scholastic.

Modern Folktales

Aldersen, B. (1997). *The swan's stories: Hans Christian Andersen*. Ill. C. Riddell. Cambridge, MA: Candlewick Press.

Andersen, H.C. (1967). *The little mermaid*. Adapted by Anthea Bell. Ill. C. Iwasaki. New York: Scholatic.

Andersen, H.C. (1971). The constant tin soldier. In *Fairy tales*. New York: Golden Pleasure Books.

Andersen, H.C. (1981). *Wild swans*. Retold by Amy Ehrlich. New York: Dial Books for Young Readers.

Andersen, H.C. (1987). *The little match girl*. Ill. R. Isadora. New York: Putnam.

Andersen, H.C. (1990). *The ugly duckling*. Ill. D. Dunlze. New York: South Books.

Andersen, H.C. (1991). *Thumbelina*. New York: Putman.

Andersen, H.C. (1994). *Twelve tales*. Ill. E. Blegvad. New York: Margaret K. McElderry Books.

Bailey, L. (1997). *Gordon Loggins and the three bears*. Buffalo, NY: Kids Can.

Berenzy, A. (1989). *A frog prince*. New York: Henry Holt and Company.

Brown, A. (1981). *Hansel and Gretel*. New York: Alfred A. Knopf.

Brown, A. (1981). *Jack and the beanstalk*. London: Walker Books Limited.

Calmenson, S. (1989). *The principal's new clothes*. New York: Scholastic.

Celsi, T. (1990). *The fourth little pig*. Milwaukee, WI: Raintree Publishers.

Cole, B. (1987). *Prince Cinders*. New York: G.P. Putnam's Sons.

French, F. (1991). *Snow White in New York*. New York: Oxford University Press.

Grahame, K. (1983). *Red riding hood*. New York: Dial Books for Young Readers.

Grahame, K. (1983). *The reluctant dragon*. New York: Henry Holt & Company.

Hooks, W.H. (1989). *The three little pigs and the wolf*. New York: Macmillan.

Marshall, J. (1987). *Red riding hood*. New York: Dial Books for Young Readers.

Marshall, J. (1988). *Goldilocks and the three bears*. New York: Dial Books for Young Readers.

Marshall, J. (1989). *The three little pigs*. New York: Dial Books for Young Readers.

McKinley, R. (1978). *Beauty: A retelling of the story of beauty and the beast*. New York: HarperCollins.

Minters, F. (1994). *Cinder-Elly*. New York: Puffin Books.

Murphy, S.R. (1977). *Silver woven in her hair*. New York: Atheneum.

Perlman, J. (1992). *Cinderella penguin*. New York: Puffin.

Perlman, J. (1994). *The emperor penguin's new clothes*. New York: Scholastic.

Scieszka, J. (1989). *The true story of the 3 little pigs*. New York: Penguin Group.

Scieszka, J. (1991). *The frog prince continued*. New York: Trumpet Book Club.

Scieszka, J., & Smith, L. (1992). *The stinky cheese man and other fairly stupid tales*. New York: Scholatic.

Thurber, J. (1990). *Many moons*. New York: Harcourt.

Tolhurst, M. (1990). *Somebody and the three Blairs*. New York: Orchard Books.

Trivizas, E. (1993). *The three little wolves and the big bad pig*. New York: Margaret K. McElderry Books.

Wolff, P. (1995). *The toll-bridge troll*. New York: Scholastic.

Yolen, J. (1972). *The girl who loved the wind*. New York: Harper Trophy.

Yolen, J. (1977). *The seeing stick*. New York: Cronwell.

Yolen, J. (1981). *Sleeping ugly*. New York: Coward–McCann.

Yolen, J. (1988). *The emperor and the kite*. New York: Philomel.

Fantasy

Adams, R. (1997). *Watership down*. New York: Thorndike Press.

Alexander, L. (1965). *The black cauldron*. New York: Henry Holt & Company.

Anderson, M.J. (1979). *In the circle of time*. New York: Alfred A. Knopf Books for Young Readers.

Anderson, M.J. (1989). *The druid's gift*. New York: Alfred A. Knopf Books for Young Readers.

Atwater, R., & Atwater, F. (1992). *Mr. Popper's penguins*. Ill. R. Lawson, Boston: Little, Brown.

Babbitt, N. (1970). *Knee knock rise*. New York: Farrar, Straus & Giroux.

Babbitt, N. (1985). *Tuck everlasting*. New York: Farrar, Straus & Giroux.

Barrie, Sir J.M. (1950). *Peter Pan*. New York: Scribner's Sons.

Bauer, M.D. (1993). *A taste of smoke*. New York: Clarion Books.

Baum, L.F. (1982). *The wizard of Oz*. New York: Henry Holt & Company.

Baum, L.F. (1996). *The wonderful wizard of Oz*. New York: NorthSouth Books.

Bianco, M.W. (1985). *The velveteen rabbit*. New York: Alfred A. Knopf Books for Young Readers.

Bond, M. (1960). *A bear called Paddington*. Boston: Houghton Mifflin.

Boston, L.M. (1989). *The children of Green Knowe*. San Diego, CA: Harcourt Brace.

Boston, L.M. (1989). *An enemy at Green Knowe*. San Diego, CA: Harcourt Brace.

Boston, L.M. (1989). *The river at Green Knowe*. San Diego, CA: Harcourt Brace.

Boston, L.M. (1989). *A stranger at Green Knowe*. San Diego, CA: Harcourt Brace.

Carroll, L. (1992). *Alice's adventures in wonderland and through the looking glass*. New York: Dell.

Christopher, J. (1967). *The white mountains*. New York: Macmillan.

Cleary, B. (1965). *The mouse and the motorcycle*. New York: Dell.

Cleary, B. (1991). *Runaway Ralph*. New York: Avon.

Collodi, C. (1989). *The adventures of Pinocchio*. New York: Simon & Schuster Children's.

Coville, B. (1989). *My teacher is an alien*. New York: Pocket Books.

Coville, B. (1997). *The skull of truth*. San Diego, CA: Harcourt Brace.

Dahl, R. (1996). *James and giant peach*. New York: Puffin.

Dahl, R. (1998). *Charlie and the chocolate factory*. New York: Alfred A. Knopf Books for Young Readers.

Fleming, I. (1964). *Chitty chitty bang bang*. New York: Random House.

Grahame, K. (1940). *The wind in the willows*. New York: Scribner's Sons.

Hahn. M.D. (1987). *Wait till Helen comes*. New York: Avon.

Hoffman, E.T.A. (1984). *The nutcracker*. New York: Crown Books.

Howe, D., & Howe, J. (1983). *Bunnicula: A rabbit tale of mystery*. New York: Atheneum.

Hurmence, B. (1982). *A girl called boy*. Boston: Houghton Mifflin.

Jacques, B. (1992). *Mariel of Redwall*. New York: Avon.

Juster, N. (1961). *The phantom tollbooth*. New York: Alfred A. Knopf Books for Young Readers.

Kendall, C. (1990). *The gammage cup*. San Diego, CA: Harcourt Brace.

King–Smith, D. (1992). *Lady Daisy*. New York: Yearling Books.

King–Smith, D. (1995). *Babe the gallant pig*. New York: Random House.

Lawson, R. (1944). *Rabbit Hill*. New York: Viking Press Children's Books.

Lawson, R. (1988). *Ben and me*. Boston: Little, Brown.

L'Engle, M. (1962). *A wrinkle in time*. New York: Farrar, Straus & Giroux.

Lewis, C.S. (1997). *The lion, the witch, & the wardrobe*. New York: HarperCollins.

Lindgren, A. (1950). *Pippi Longstocking*. New York: Viking Press Childen's Books.

Lindgren, A. (1959). *Pippi in the South Seas*. New York: Viking Press Children's Books.

Lowry, L. (1997). *The giver*. New York: Dell.

McCaffrey, A. (1994). *Dragonsong*. New York: Bantam.

McGraw, E. (1996). *The moorchild*. New York: Margaret K. McElderry Books.

Milne, A.A. (1956). *The house at pooh corner*. New York: NAL/Dutton.

Milne, A.A. (1961). *Winnie-the-pooh*. New York: NAL/Dutton.

Norton, M. (1953). *The borrowers*. San Diego, CA: Harcourt Brace.

Norton, M. (1990). *Bed-knobs and broomsticks*. Boston: Harcourt Brace.

Norton, A. (1985). *Red hart magic*. New York: Ace Books.

O'Brien, R.C. (1971). *Mrs. Frisby and the rats of NIMH*. New York: Simon & Schuster Children's.

Pinkwater, D.M. (1992). *Guys from space*. New York: Simon & Schuster Children's.

Potter, B. (1991). *The tale of Peter Rabbit*. New York: Simon & Schuster Children's.

Rowling, J.K. (1997). *Harry Potter and the sorceror's stone*. New York: Scholastic.

Rowling, J.K. (1998). *Harry Potter and the chamber of secrets*. New York: Scholastic.

Rowling, J.K. (1999). *Harry Potter and the prisoner of Azkaban*. New York: Scholastic.

Selden, G. (1996). *The cricket in Times Square*. New York: Dell.

Slaughter, H. (1993). *Windmill Hill*. New York: Pippin Press.

Swift, J. (1997). *Gulliver's travels*. Anaheim, CA: BNI Publications.

Tolkien, J.R.R. (1997). *The hobbit*. Boston: Houghton Mifflin.

Travers, P.L. (1962). *Mary Poppins*. New York: Harcourt Brace.

Van Allsburg, C. (1981). *Jumanji*. Boston: Houghton Mifflin.

Van Allsburg, C. (1983). *The wreck of the zephyr*. Boston: Houghton Mifflin.

White, E.B. (1945). *Stuart Little*. New York: HarperCollins Children's Books.

White, E.B. (1952). *Charlotte's web*. New York: HarperCollins Children's Books.

White, E.B. (1970). *The trumpet of the swan*. New York: HarperCollins Children's Books.

Winthrop, E. (1985). *The castle in the attic*. New York: Bantam.

Winthrop, E. (1993). *The battle for the castle*. New York: Holiday House.

Yolen, J. (1984). *Dragon's blood*. New York: Dell.

Yolen, J. (1990). *Devil's arithmetic*. New York: Puffin.

Biographies

Adler, D. (1989). *A picture book of Abraham Lincoln*. New York: Trumpet Club.

Adler, D. (1989). *A picture book of George Washington*. New York: Trumpet Club.

Adler, D. (1990). *A picture book of Benjamin Franklin*. New York: Trumpet Club.

Adler, D. (1992). *A picture book of Harriet Tubman*. New York: Holiday House.

Adler, D. (1998). *A picture book of Amelia Earhart*. New York: Holiday House.

Adoff, A. (1970). *Malcolm X*. Ill. by J. Wilson. New York: HarperCollins.

Anderson, W. (1992). *Laura Ingalls Wilder: A biography*. New York: HarperCollins.

Bains, R. (1982). *Harriet Tubman: The road to freedom*. New York: Troll.

Banta, M. (1993). *Frederick Douglass: Voice of liberty*. Lebanon, NH: Chelsea House Publishers.

Black, S. (1989). *Sitting Bull and the Battle of the Little Bighorn*. New York: Silver Burdett.

Blumberg, R. (1993). *Bloomers!* New York: Macmillan.

Bolden, T. (1998). *And not afraid to dare: Stories of ten African American women*. New York: Scholastic.

Brenner, M. (1994). *Abe Lincoln's hat*. New York: Scholastic.

Brewster, H. (1996). *Anastasia's album*. Westport, CT: Hyperion Books for Children.

Brooks, P.S. (1983). *Queen Eleanor: Independent spirit of the medieval world*. New York: Lippincott.

Burch, J. (1994). *A fairy-tale life: A story about Hans Christian Andersen*. Minneapolis, MN: Carolrhoda Books.

Cha, D. (1996). *Dia's story cloth: The Hmong people's journey to freedom*. New York: Lee & Low.

Clifton, G. (1995). *Charles A. Lindbergh: A human hero*. Ill. by D. DiSalvo-Ryan. New York: Clarion Books.

Clifton, G. (1995). *Mr. Lincoln's drummer*. New York: Scholastic.

Collins, D.R. (1989). *To the point: A story about E.B. White*. Minneapolis, MN: Carolrhoda Books, Inc.

Collins, M. (1976). *Flying to the moon and other strange places*. New York: Farrar, Straus & Giroux.

Conklin, T. (1994). *Steven Spielberg*. New York: Random House.

Davidson, M. (1969). *Helen Keller*. New York: Scholastic.

Davidson, M. (1981). *The Golda Meir story*. New York: Scribner's Sons.

Davis, O. (1978). *Escape to freedom: A play about young Frederick Douglas*. New York: Puffin.

DeKay, J.T. (1969). *Meet Martin Luther King, Jr.* New York: Random House.

Fisher, L.E. (1990). *Prince Henry the Navigator*. New York: Macmillan.

Fisher, L.E. (1994). *Marie Curie*. New York: Macmillan.

Ford, A. (1988). *John James Audubon*. New York: Abbeville Press.

Fradin, D.B. (1992). *Hiawatha: Messenger of peace*. New York: MacMillan.

Freedman, R. (1987). *Lincoln: A Photobiography*. New York: Scholastic.

Freedman, R. (1991). *The Wright Brothers: How they invented the airplane*. New York: Holiday House.

Freedman, R. (1993). *Eleanor Roosevelt: A life of discovery*. New York: Clarion.

Fritz, J. (1969). *George Washington's breakfast*. New York: Coward-McCann.

Fritz, J. (1973). *And then what happened Paul Revere?* New York: Coward-McCann.

Fritz, J. (1976). *What's the big idea Ben Franklin?* New York: Coward-McCann.

Fritz, J. (1976). *Will you sign here, John Hancock?* New York: Coward-McCann.

Fritz, J. (1977). *Can't you make them behave, King George?* New York: Coward-McCann.

Fritz, J. (1980). *Where do you think you're going, Christopher Columbus?* New York: Coward-McCann.

Fritz, J. (1983). *The double life of Pocahontas*. New York: Trumpet Club.

Fritz, J. (1991). *Bully for you, Teddy Roosevelt!* Ill. by M. Wemmer. New York: G.P. Putnam's Sons.

Fritz, J. (1992). *George Washington's mother*. Ill. by D. DiSalvo–Ryan. New York: Scholastic.

Gherman, B. (1992). *E.B. White: Some writer!* New York: Atheneum.

Graff, S., & P.A. (1991). *Helen Keller: Crusader for the blind and deaf*. New York: Bantam Doubleday Dell.

Green, C. (1989). *Ludwig Van Beethoven*. Chicago: Children's Press.

Green, C. (1990). *Laura Ingalls Wilder: Author of the little house books*. Chicago: Children's Press.

Green, C. (1991). *Hans Christian Andersen: Prince of storytellers*. Chicago: Children's Press.

Green, C. (1992). *John Philip Sousa*. Chicago: Children's Press.

Green, C. (1995). *L. Frank Baum: Author of the Wonderful Wizard of Oz*. Chicago: Children's Press.

Haber, L. (1970). *Black pioneers of science and invention*. Orlando, FL: Harcourt Brace.

Hall, D. (1996). *When Willard met Babe Ruth*. San Diego, CA: Harcourt Brace.

Harrison, B., & Terris, D. (1992). *A twilight struggle: The life of John Fitzgerald Kennedy*. New York: Lothrop, Lee & Shepard.

Houston, G. (1992). *My great aunt Arizona*. New York: HarperCollins.

Hudson, W. (1995a). *Five brave explorers*. New York: Scholastic.

Hudson, W. (1995b). *Five notable inventors*. New York: Scholastic.

Jakes, J. (1986). *Susanna of the Alamo*. New York: Harcourt Brace Jovanovich.

Keegan, M. (1991). *Pueblo boy: Growing up in two worlds*. New York: Cobblehill Books.

Krull, K. (1996). *Wilma unlimited: How Wilma Rudolph became the fastest woman in the world*. San Diego, CA: Harcourt Brace.

Lasky, K. (1998). *A brilliant streak: The making of Mark Twain*. San Diego, CA: Harcourt Brace.

Latham, J.L. (1955). *Carry on, Mr. Boditch*. New York: Houghton Mifflin.

Lepscky, I. (1984). *Pablo Picasso*. New York: Trumpet Club.

Lepscky, I. (1990). *Marie Curie*. New York: Trumpet Club.

Lester, J. (1994). *John Henry*. New York: Dial Books.

Levinson, N.S. (1992). *Snowshoe Thompson*. Ill. by J. Sandin. New York: HarperCollins.

Littlefield, B. (1993). *Stories of ten remarkable athletes*. New York: Little, Brown.

Lowery, L. (1996a). *Georgia O'Keefe*. Minneapolis, MN: Carolrhoda.

Lowery, L. (1996b). *Wilma Mankiller*. Minneapolis, MN: Carolrhoda.

Lyons, M.E. (1993). *Starting home: The story of Horace Pippin, painter*. New York: Scribner.

McGovern, A. (1965). *Wanted dead or alive: The true story of Harriet Tubman.* New York: Scholastic.

McKissack, P., & McKissack, F. (1992). *Rebels against slavery: American slave revolts.* New York: Scholastic.

McKissack, P., & McKissack, F. (1992). *Sojourner Truth: Ain't I a woman?* New York: Scholastic.

McKissack, P., & McKissack, F. (1998). *Young, black, and determined: A biography of Lorraine Hansberry.* New York: Holiday House.

McMullan, K. (1991). *The story of Harriet Tubman: Conductor of the Underground Railroad.* New York: Bantam Doubleday Dell.

McPherson, S. (1992). *I speak for the women: A story about Lucy Stone.* Minneapolis, MN: Carolrhoda.

Medearis, A. (1997). *Princess of the press: The story of Ida B. Wells-Barnett.* New York: Lodestary Dutton.

Monjo, F.N. (1973). *Me and Willie and Pa: The story of Abraham Lincoln and his son Tad.* New York: Simon & Schuster.

Monjo, F.N. (1990). *Grand Papa and Ellen Aroon.* New York: Dell.

Myers, W.D. (1996). *Toussaint L' ouverture: The fight for Haiti's freedom.* New York, NY: Simon & Schuster.

Nichol, B. (1993). *Beethoven lives upstairs.* New York: Orchard Books.

Orgill, R. (1997). *If I only had a horn: Young Louis Armstrong.* Boston: Houghton Mifflin.

Osofsky, A. (1996). *Free to dream: The making of a poet Langston Hughes.* New York: Lothrop, Lee & Shepard.

Pinkney, A.D. (1993). *Alvin Ailey.* Boston: Hyperion.

Pinkney, A.D. (1996). *Bill Pickett: Rodeo-ridin' cowboy.* San Diego, CA: Harcourt Brace.

Porter, A.P. (1992). *Jump at de sun: The story of Zora Neale Hurston.* Minneapolis, MN: Carolrhoda.

Pringle, L. (1991). *Batman: Exploring the world of bats.* New York: Scribner.

Raschka, C. (1992). *Charlie Parker played be bop.* Boston: Orchard/Richard Jackson.

Rinaldi, A. (1996). *Hang a thousand trees with ribbons: The story of Phyllis Wheatly.* San Diego, CA: Harcourt Brace.

Roessel, M. (1995). *Songs from the loom: A Navajo girl learns to weave.* Minneapolis, MN: Lerner Publications.

Ryan, C. (1993). *Louisa May Alcott: Her girlhood diary.* New York: Troll Medallion.

Say, A. (1990). *El chino.* New York: Houghton Mifflin.

Schroeder, A. (1996). *Satchmo's blues.* New York: Doubleday.

Schwartz, D.M. (1991). *Supergrandpa*. New York: Lothrop, Lee & Shepard.

Seldon, B. (1989). *The story of Walt Disney: Maker of magical worlds*. New York: Bantom Doubleday Dell.

Sherrow, V. (1992). *Phyllis Wheatley—Poet*. Lebanon, NH: Chelsea House.

Smith, K. (1987). *Abraham Lincoln*. New York: Scholastic.

St. George, J. (1992). *Dear Dr. Bell...Your friend, Helen Keller*. New York: Putnam.

Stanley, D. (1996). *Leonardo Da Vinci*. New York: Morrow.

Stanley, D., & Vennema, P. (1992a). *Bard of Avon: The story of William Shakespeare*. New York: Morrow.

Stanley, D. & Vennema, P. (1992b). *Cleopatra*. New York: Morrow.

Stanley, F. (1991). *The last princess: The story of Princess Kaiulani of Hawaii*. New York: Aladdin Books.

Stanley, J. (1992). *Children of the Dust Bowl: The true story of the school at Weedpatch Camp*. New York: Trumpet Book Club.

Stine, M. (1992). *The story of Laura Ingalls Wilder, pioneer girl*. New York: Dell.

Swanson, G.M., & Swanson, M.V. (1994). *I've got an idea: The story of Frederick McKinley Jones*. Minneapolis, MN: Runeston Press/Lerner.

Towle, W. (1993). *The real McCoy; The life of a African-American inventor*. New York: Scholastic.

Turner, R. (1991). *Georgia O'Keefe*. Boston: Little, Brown.

Van der Rol, R., & Verhoeven, R. (1993). *Anne Frank, beyond the diary: A photographic remembrance*. New York: Viking.

Venezia, M. (1951). *George Gershwin: Getting to know the world's greatest composers*. Chicago: Children's Press.

Weidt, M. (1994). *Oh, the places he went: A story about Dr. Seuss*. Minneapolis, MN: Carolrhoda Books.

Wetterer, M. (1990). *Kate Shelley and the midnight express*. Minneapolis, MN: Carolrhoda Books.

Wetterer, M.K. & Wetterer, C.M. (1996). *The snow walker*. Minneapolis, MN: Carolrhoda Books.

Zhensun, Z., & Low, A. (1991). *A young painter: The life and paintings of Wang Yani-China's extraordinary young artist*. New York: Scholastic Books.

Autobiographies and Memoirs

Bean, A. (1988). *My life: Tales of childhood*. New York: Farrar, Straus & Giroux.

Bulla, C. (1985). *A grain of wheat: A writer begins*. New York: David R. Godine.

Byars, B. (1991). *The moon and I*. New York: Messner.

Cleary, B. (1988). *A girl from Yamhill: A memoir*. New York: Morrow.

Dahl, R. (1984). *Boy: Tales of childhood*. New York: Farrar, Straus & Giroux.

DePaola, T. (1989). *The art lesson*. New York: Putnam.

Duncan, L. (1982). *Chapters: My growth as a writer*. Boston: Little, Brown.

Gish, L. (1987). *An actor's life for me!* New York: Viking.

Goodall, J. (1988). *My life with the chimpanzees*. New York: Simon & Schuster.

Fritz, J. (1982). *Homesick: My own story*. New York: Putnam.

Huynh, Q.N. (1992). *The land I lost: Adventures of a boy in Vietnam*. New York: HarperCollins.

Hyman, T.S. (1981). *Self-portrait: Trina Schart Hyman*. New York: Addison–Wesley.

Keller, H. (1980). *The story of my life*. New York: Watermill Press.

King–Smith, D. (1997). *Puppy love*. Cambridge, MA: Candlewick.

Naylor, P.R. (1987). *How I came to be a writer*. New York: Aladdin.

O'Kelly, M.L. (1980). *From the hills of Georgia: An autobiography in paintings*. Boston: Little, Brown.

Paulsen, G. (1993). *Eastern sun, winter moon: An autobiographical essay*. San Diego, CA: Harcourt Brace.

Paulsen, G. (1995). *Winterdance: The fine madness of running the Iditarod*. San Diego, CA: Harcourt Brace.

Peet, B. (1989). *Bill Peet: An autobiography*. Boston: Houghton Mifflin.

Rylant, C. (1985). *The relatives came*. New York: Bradbury Press.

Rylant, C. (1989). *But I'll be back again: An album*. New York: Orchard Books.

Rylant, C. (1992a). *Best Wishes*. Photographs by C. Ontal. Katonah, NY: Richard C. Owen.

Rylant, C. (1992b). *When I was young in the mountains*. New York: Dutton.

Schulz, C.M. (1980). *Charlie Brown, Snoopy and me: And all the other Peanuts characters*. New York: Doubleday.

Uchida, Y. (1991). *The invisible tread*. New York: Messner.

Yep, L. (1991). *The lost garden*. New York: Messner.

Yolen, J. (1987). *Owl moon*. New York: Philomel.

Yolen, J. (1992). *A letter from Phoenix Farm*. Katonah, NJ: Richard C. Owen.

Web Sites

Children's Literature (General)

The following Web sites contain links to genres of children's literature, authors and illustrators, and teacher resources.

Children's Literature Site
http://www.childrenlit.com
All about children's literature and features Children's Literature Choices, Meet the Authors and Illustrators, and teaching materials. Featured authors include Virginia Hamilton, Dick King–Smith, Kathryn Laskey, Avi, Joseph Bruchac, Jan Britt, Patricia McKissack, Cynthia Rylant, Louis Sachar, and more.

Children's Literature Resource Page
http://www.acs.ucalgary.ca/dkbrown/index.html
Features The Book Read Project and BR, which matches classrooms to discuss books. Contains lesson plans for Cinderella, and ideas for teaching Cinderella variants. Also ideas for Readers Theatre.

The Children's Literature Web Guide
http://www.ucalgary.ca/~dkbrown/
Comprehensive Web site guide for children's literature. Contains online children's stories (folktales like Cinderella and contemprary stories), and links to book recommendations, book awards, book publishers, author sites, resources for teachers and parents, and other children's literature Web sites.

ISLMC Children's Literature & Language Arts Resources
http://falcon.jmu.edu/ramseyil/childlit.htm
The (Internet School Library Media Center) ISLMC provides information about authors and illustrators, genres, book awards, literacy enrichment activities (like storytelling and Readers Theatre), curriculum resources, and links to other children's literature Web sites.

Carol Hurst's Children's Literature Site
http://www.carolhurst.com
Contains reviews of children's books (by title, author, or type of book), and author sites that include a short biographical sketch and annotated bibliography of the author's books. Also gives suggestions for author studies, themes, curricular connections, and links to other children's literature sites.

KidsClick! Children's Author Web Site
http://sunsite.berkeley.edu/KidsClick!/toplite.html
Created by librarians especially for kids. Students can use a keyword, title, or author to search a specific genre. This search will give results that include a brief synopsis of the book. There are also links to general author sites, individual author sites, and a book list.

Children's Authors
http://www.sir.arizona.edu/Sp97/560/web/AdultLit/authors.htm
Features the authors Lois Duncan, Avi, Virginia Hamilton, and Katherine Paterson.

Genre-Specific Web sites

Realistic Fiction and Fantasy

Project Guttenberg
http://www.promo.net/pg
Gives full text of stories, such as *Alice in Wonderland.*

Mysteries

The four Web sites below are part of the MysteryNet.com, an online mystery network, found at *http://MysteryNet.com.*

The Case.com for Kids
http://www.TheCase.com/kids/
Contains online weekly mini–mysteries (called Solve–it) that students can solve via e–mail, a quick–solve mystery, a free monthly writing contest, and links to other mystery sites.

Nancy Drew
http://NancyDrew.com
Allows students to read and react to Nancy Drew books online. Opportunities for students to discuss books and episodes via e–mail. Provides lesson plans designed for teaching the mystery genre, including vocabulary, comprehension and mystery–writing exercises. Gives links to other mystery sites, as well.

Learning with Mysteries
http://www.MysteryNet.com/learn/lessonplans/mystery.html
Includes resources for teachers who want to use mysteries in the classroom for grades 4 and up. Lessons include information about the mystery genre, and exercises to enrich vocabulary, solve the mystery, teach elements of the genre, and help students to write a mystery. Provides links to other mystery sites.

Mystery Writers of America
http://www.MysteryNet.com/mwa

To stay up–to–date on the best children's mysteries, teachers can visit this site for the Mystery Writers of America. Each year this organization awards the Edgar Award for the Best Children's Mystery and lists the winner of this award and the nominees.

Traditional and Modern Folktales

Tales of Wonder
http://members.xoom.com/darsie/tales/index.html
Contains folktales from around the world. Stories listed on the main page by country of origin. Each tale has its own Web page.

Indigenous People's Literature
http://www.indians.org/Resource/resource.html
Contains Native American folktales, fables, and contemporary fiction listed by topic (bears, eagles, etc.) and includes the nation of origin. A valuable resource for teachers, the real strength of this site is the section of book reviews and recommendations; the "thumbs up" icon indicates books that are free from racism, factual inaccuracies, and misleading statements.

Biographies

Biography.com
http://biography.com/class/classroom.html
A database of over 20,000 biographies of people of the past and the present. Lists a weekly program calendar for the school year plus study guides for using the programs found on the Biography Channel and History Channel. Teachers are also encouraged to tape the programs and use the materials in the classroom. Includes links to other biography sites.

Student Writing

Inkspot
http://www.inkspot/com
Interactive Web site on which students can post their writing and meet an online peer–critique partner with whom to exchange works in progress.

Reading-Related Sites

The Reading Dimension
http://www.eduplace.com/kids/book/index.html
Sponsored by Houghton Mifflin, an interactive site where students can share books online (KidViews) and have online discussions (Kids to Kids Discussion) of select titles that the company features.

World of Reading
http://www.worldreading.org
A "safe" site for students to submit reviews of books and to read the reviews of other students. Students can search for a specific book by title or author, then read the review or submit their own.

Index

Note: An *f* following a page number indicates that the reference may be found in a figure.

A

GUIDED READING, SMALL-GROUP: of biographies, 144–145; of fables, 93–94; of fantasy, 125–126; of modern folktales, 107–108; of mystery stories, 45; of pourquoi stories, 84–86; of realistic fiction, 26; of traditional folktales, 69–71

H

HABER, LOUIS, 172; *Black Pioneers of Science and Invention*, 135
HADDIX, M.P., 159
HAGUE, MICHAEL, 166; *Aesop's Fables*, 90, 91
HAHN, MARY DOWNING, 159, 169; *The Dead Man in Indian Creek*, 34
HALL, D., 172
HALL, LYNN, 159; *The Tormentors*, 34
HAMILTON, VIRGINIA, 159; *The House of Dies Drear*, 34
HARPER, W., 161
HARRISON, B., 172
HARSTE, J., 2, 153
HAYES, S., 161
HEINS, P., 161
HELPER, S., 32, 56, 99, 132, 153
HENRY, M., 156
HERMAN, H., 158
HERZIG, A.C., 159
HICKMAN, J., 32, 56, 99, 114, 132, 153
HICKOX, R., 161
HILDICK, E.W., 159; *Hester Bidgood, Investigatrix of Evil Deeds*, 33
HILL, K., 157
HILLMAN, J., 7, 57, 99, 153
HISER, C., 158
HISTORICAL REALISTIC FICTION, 8
HISTORICAL BIOGRAPHIES, 136
HISTORICAL MYSTERIES, 33
HMONG (LAOS) TALES, 56–57, 60
HOFFMAN, E.T.A., 168
HOFFMAN, MARY, 156; *Amazing Grace*, 136
HOLCOMB, J.K., 157
HOOKS, W.H., 161, 167
HOUSTON, GLORIA, 172; *My Great Aunt Arizona*, 145
HOWE, DEBORAH, 169; *Bunnicula: A Rabbit Tale of Mystery*, 117
HOWE, JAMES, 33, 154, 169; *Bunnicula: A Rabbit Tale of Mystery*, 117

V

W

47–53; Pourquoi Maps, 85–86, 85f, 86–87; of pourquoi stories, 85–87; process, 2; questions for, 29, 52–53, 76, 88, 96, 111, 129–131, 148; of realistic fiction, 26–29; of traditional folktales, 71–76; Web sites for, 179